What is Grounded Theory?

'What is?' Research Methods Series
Edited by Graham Crow

The 'What is?' series provides authoritative introductions to a range of research methods which are at the forefront of developments in the social sciences. Each volume sets out the key elements of the particular method and features examples of its application, drawing on a consistent structure across the whole series. Written in an accessible style by leading experts in the field, this series is an innovative pedagogical and research resource.

What are Community Studies?
Graham Crow

What is Diary Method?
Ruth Bartlett and Christine Milligan

What is Discourse Analysis?
Stephanie Taylor

What is Inclusive Research?
Melanie Nind

What is Narrative Research?
Molly Andrews, Mark Davis, Cigdem Esin, Lar-Christer Hyden, Margareta Hyden, Corinne Squire and Barbara Harrison

What is Online Research?
Tristram Hooley, Jane Wellens and John Marriott

What is Qualitative Interviewing?
Rosalind Edwards and Janet Holland

What is Qualitative Research?
Martyn Hammersley

What are Qualitative Research Ethics?
Rose Wiles

What is Social Network Analysis?
John Scott

What is Qualitative Longitudinal Research?
Bren Neale

What is Rhythmanalysis?
Dawn Lyon

Forthcoming books:

What is Statistical Modelling in R?
Kevin Ralston, Vernon Gayle, Roxanne Connelly and Chris Playford

What is grounded theory?

Massimiliano Tarozzi

BLOOMSBURY ACADEMIC
LONDON • NEW YORK • OXFORD • NEW DELHI • SYDNEY

BLOOMSBURY ACADEMIC
Bloomsbury Publishing Plc
50 Bedford Square, London, WC1B 3DP, UK
1385 Broadway, New York, NY 10018, USA

BLOOMSBURY, BLOOMSBURY ACADEMIC and the Diana logo are trademarks of Bloomsbury Publishing Plc

First published in Great Britain 2020

Series design by Paul Burgess
Cover image © Shutterstock

A catalogue record for this book is available from the British Library.

Library of Congress Cataloging-in-Publication Data
Names: Tarozzi, Massimiliano, author.
Title: What is grounded theory? / Massimiliano Tarozzi.
Description: London, UK; New York, NY: Bloomsbury Academic, 2020. |
Series: The 'what is?' research methods series | Includes bibliographical references and index.
Identifiers: LCCN 2020018633 (print) | LCCN 2020018634 (ebook) |
ISBN 9781350085237 (paperback) | ISBN 9781350085244 (hardback) |
ISBN 9781350085268 (ebook) | ISBN 9781350085251 (epub)
Subjects: LCSH: Grounded theory.
Classification: LCC H61.24 .T37 2020 (print) | LCC H61.24 (ebook) | DDC 001.4/2–dc23

LC record available at https://lccn.loc.gov/2020018633
LC ebook record available at https://lccn.loc.gov/2020018634

ISBN: HB: 978-1-3500-8524-4
PB: 978-1-3500-8523-7
ePDF: 978-1-3500-8526-8
eBook: 978-1-3500-8525-1

Series: The 'What is?' Research Methods Series

Typeset by Deanta Global Publishing Services, Chennai, India

To find out more about our authors and books visit www.bloomsbury.com and sign up for our newsletters.

Contents

Series Editor's Foreword

The idea behind this series is a simple one: to provide concise and accessible overviews of a range of frequently used research methods and of current issues in research methodology. Books in the series have been written by experts in their fields with a brief to write about their subject for a broad audience who are assumed to be interested but not necessarily to have any prior knowledge. The series is a natural development of presentations made in the 'What is?' strand at Economic and Social Research Council Research Methods Festivals which have proved popular both at the Festivals themselves and subsequently as a resource on the website of the ESRC National Centre for Research Methods.

Methodological innovation is the order of the day, and the 'What is?' format allows researchers who are new to a field to gain an insight into its key features, while also providing a useful update on recent developments for people who have had some prior acquaintance with it. All readers should find it helpful to be taken through the discussion of key terms, the history of how the method or methodological issue has developed and the assessment of the strengths and possible weaknesses of the approach through analysis of illustrative examples.

This fourteenth book in the series is devoted to Grounded Theory (GT). In it, Massimiliano Tarozzi provides a compelling account of an approach that has come to be remarkably influential in the five decades since Barney Glaser and Anselm Strauss published *The Discovery of Grounded Theory* in 1967. This is a story with several facets. One of these is the adoption of GT by researchers in a wide range of disciplines, including disciplines related to health, as well retaining a strong grounding in its originators' home discipline, sociology. A second facet is that, like all innovations, GT has not stood still but has developed in various directions, including ones that are antithetical. As a result, profound disagreements have emerged about how best to characterize GT and also how to practise it, although with sufficient common ground retained to warrant continued use of the term to denote a recognizably distinctive approach. Despite the differences that have emerged over the years about how best to employ GT in a research project, all of its adherents agree that it is not a method that promises a quick fix to the challenges of the research process; it is not, therefore, for the faint hearted. Tarozzi's openness about his own moments of frustration, self-doubt and exhaustion provides a candid reminder of how hard the struggle to make sense of the social world can be. Such stories are, however, more than balanced by the sense of achievement and of exhilaration that accompany the arrival at the enlightening resolution of a problem with which one has grappled. Furthermore, grounded theorists are generally engaged in such struggles in pursuit of a solution that will be of benefit to others, and the author conveys nicely the sense of collective appreciation that can accompany such moments of resolution.

The books in this series cannot provide information about their subject matter down to a fine level of detail, but they will equip readers with a powerful sense of reasons why it deserves to be taken seriously and, it is hoped, with the enthusiasm to put that knowledge into practice.

Graham Crow

Preface

When I submitted my PhD thesis in the mid-1990s, I received a friendly, pointed and pertinent critique from a colleague. My thesis presented a theoretical analysis built on the foundations of a field of study which at the time remained largely unexplored, that is, intercultural education; this was followed by an empirical inquiry into the functions and role of cultural mediators in Italian schools. The empirical component consisted of narrative autobiographical interviews with one of the first cultural mediators working in Bologna, supported by observations using shadowing technique. I studied this professional for several months as he carried out his activities in numerous schools in the province. The two parts of the thesis, theoretical and empirical, were completely disjointed. However, I used some theoretical interpretative categories that had emerged from the first part to analyse and interpret the empirical data in the second part. When I went to analyse the enormous amounts of very rich data I had collected, I was faced with the classic dilemma of the qualitative researcher: How can I make sense of all this data that I have so far only systematized and organized in a merely descriptive form?

Since the categories of equality, difference and relationship had emerged from the theoretical part as the fundamental dimensions of a pedagogically founded intercultural education, I used mainly those three categories to pedagogically interpret the empirical data I had collected. They actually worked quite well, in fact, enabling me to add a further chapter on the 'value in use' of my research. Later, my thesis was published as a book (Tarozzi, 1998).

My brilliant doctoral colleague criticized my choice to apply theoretical interpretative categories to empirical analysis, however, calling it 'Kantian'. This appellation wounded me deeply and hurt my pride as a field researcher. To apply interpretive schemes based on a purely speculative reflection on reality is a philosophical-idealistic act. Not anything bad in itself, but inadequate when it comes to doing (qualitative) empirical research. I tried to explain to my colleague that, from a phenomenological perspective, the theoretical horizon in which we both positioned ourselves, this act was perfectly legitimate. In the end I did not convince either of us, however, and that adjective 'Kantian' stuck with me for quite a while.

And so, when carrying out my next research for a post-doc fellowship and again having to work with large amounts of qualitative data, I chose to seek interpretive categories constructed beginning from the data.

It was at that point, in looking for methodological support for this approach, that I first came across Glaser and Strauss's text *The Discovery of Grounded Theory*. The aspect of this method that immediately struck me was the possibility of making qualitative data analysis embedded, rooted or, to use the authors' term, *grounded* in the data.

I present this autobiographical episode as an introduction to the text to highlight two characteristics that prove quite influential for understanding the essence of this method and perhaps beginning to develop a passion for it. The first characteristic is the unique opportunity to build analytical categories starting from the data and, therefore, to be faithful to the phenomenon and to respect it by following the indications that come directly from it. The second is the possibility to combine empirical and theoretical research. Few research methodologies aim at theory building, not even through 'middle-range' theories. Kathy Charmaz has observed that a fundamental feature of the GT method is that it allows us to 'explicitly unite the research process with theoretical development. Hence, the rigid division of labour between empiricists and theorists breaks down' (Charmaz, 1995, p. 28).

Following its inception in 1967, GT has come to represent one of the most widely used and popular qualitative research methods (Bryant & Charmaz, 2007) across a wide range of disciplines. A simple search of the influential worldwide database ISI Web of Science shows that, in 2007–17, almost 12,000 articles have been published in major scholarly journals claiming to use GT. While in 1980 only thirty studies used GT, by 2017 the number of such articles had risen to 1,686. Of course, there have been annual increments in the number of journals included in the data base ISI Web of Science. This growth curve is nonetheless noticeable and significant, however, with no other qualitative methods enjoying such a meteoric trajectory. The use of GT methodology has increased over the years, and, especially in the last decade, it has also been broadly applied worldwide, beyond the country (United States) in which it was generated.

Such a growing number of GT articles, indexed in a major scholarly database, demonstrates that GT is becoming an appealing and perhaps even fashionable approach across the world. It is also noticeable that GT is currently used in a number of different fields and disciplines other than those in which it was developed (sociology) and originally applied (nursing and health sciences). Indeed, GT has been used in a wide range of disciplines and different research domains such as nursing, computer science, marketing, psychology, education, management, family studies and women's studies.

Nursing was certainly a pioneering field for the use of GT. According to Benoliel (1996), in a historically oriented special issue on 'Qualitative Health Research' devoted to 'diffusion, diluition, or distillation. The case of GT', its influence on knowledge generation in nursing began in the 1960s and expanded over the following two decades. In particular, in the 'decade of diffusion' (1980–90), GT research carried out by nurses spread worldwide and increased greatly in scope and differentiation. In other disciplines outside the health sciences, the GT peak occurred in the first decade of this century.

Arguably, references to GT are very often vague and sometimes incorrect. Many, too many, researchers limit their description of how they used it to a generic mention of theory building, an inductive approach, or the use of GT jargon but not necessarily its procedures (Glaser, 2009). As I seek to show in this book, however, GT has its own specific nature and procedures. Throughout the following chapters I will present the procedures of GT as if they were singular and unanimously accepted. As Charmaz has clearly shown, over the last fifty years this method has been developed along so many different pathways that she has defined it as a 'constellation of methods'.

Nevertheless, without the pretence of presenting a definitive or authentic perspective, I introduce GT procedures as I have applied and mastered them over the twenty years of my research and teaching.

The aim of this book is essentially pragmatic, that is, to illustrate how to do GT; I will not, therefore, dwell excessively on theoretical debates, but instead will outline the key literature for anyone wishing to explore these discussions in greater depth.

I agree with Birks and Mills (2010) when they maintain that researchers planning to use GT should position themselves in the context of various GT traditions and, more broadly, within the framework of various ontological and epistemological perspectives by framing their assumptions through existing worldviews and paradigms.

In this book I have decided not to take sides, however, avoiding the kind of parochial approach that is one of the reasons for the rigid, narrow and sometimes dogmatic ways some people introduce GT. I will certainly underscore diversity in GT approaches, procedures and even goals, but I prefer to stress the commonalities among different schools over their divergences. Over the years I have had the opportunity to meet and collaborate with most of the grounded theorists belonging to different schools. I wrote up a conversation with Barney Glaser (2007), contributed to Corbin's book (Corbin & Strauss, 2015), collaborated with Charmaz on several projects and was invited by her and Adele Clarke to contribute to a book they edited (Clarke & Charmaz, 2014) and again by her and Anthony Bryant to collaborate to their successful handbook (Bryant & Charmaz, 2019). Based on my personal experience, I could potentially find strengths and key elements in each one of these versions. Of course my view is not neutral nor indifferent. Rather, I endorse a phenomenological horizon as the theoretical framework underlying my presentation of GT. This positioning also allows me to avoid the trap of rigid and dogmatic viewpoints and instead appreciate the valuable contributions from different GT schools.

In the first three chapters, under the section 'Understanding GT', I recursively address the nature of this method on different levels: its definition, its story and its processual dimension, with a brief mention of its epistemological level. This will allow me to deploy different perspectives to shed light on the same complex object in the hope that the partial illumination of its parts will generate an understanding of the whole.

The last three chapters, under 'Doing GT', aim to accompany the research process through its various phases, focusing on practical methodological nodes. I am aware that one does not learn a research method just by reading a short introduction or even an extensive handbook about it; however, I am also convinced that explaining *how to do* GT might just be the best way to understand *what it is*.

It is no coincidence that this book originates from two decades of research practice and teaching. Teaching qualitative research methodology courses and GT seminars to students motivated to learn the method so that they might apply it has been incredibly stimulating and productive.

This book is dedicated to all my postgraduate students without whose competent and active contribution, not to mention their constant and critical stimulus, this book would never have seen the light of day.

Acknowledgements

A special thank you to Dr. Romina De Angelis and Dr. Angelina Zontine for their support in editing some chapters of this book.

Part I
Understanding GT

1 What Is Grounded Theory?

1.1 Starting from the Definition of Grounded Theory

In 1967, Barney Glaser and Anselm Strauss published *The Discovery of Grounded Theory* presenting the first formulation of an innovative method for conducting qualitative research. The introduction to this text featured a concise definition of this approach. I do not particularly like definitions, however, it is convenient to begin with the following one by deconstructing it into some important keywords that shed light on the features and distinctive traits of this method.

> Grounded theory is a *general method* of comparative analysis (…) and a *set of procedures* able to generate [*systematically*] a theory *grounded in the data*. (Glaser & Strauss, 1967, p. viii, emphasis added)

1) A *general method*. According to its founders, Grounded Theory (GT) can be regarded as 'a general method' (elsewhere defined as 'strategic method', p. 21) for generating a theory and at the same time as 'a set of procedures'. It is a methodology, namely an overall rational discourse or way of thinking about (or constructing) social reality, or to draw on Michael Crotty (2015), it is the strategy, the plan of action, the process underlying the choice and use of particular methods. At the same time, however, it is also a method, that is to say a procedure, a *techne*, a set of techniques or tools, used to gather, treat and analyse data (Cohen, Manion & Morrison, 2018). Reflecting on one's methodological approach should account for the process of *investigative* work while the method is functional to the researcher's *productive* work.
2) *Set of procedures*. Since that first definition, different views have been put forward over time as to how GT should be understood and positioned among methods or methodologies. For Glaser (1978) and others it is essentially a methodology; for Juliet Corbin (Strauss & Corbin, 1990) and recently, Bryant (2017), it is a method;

for Kathy Charmaz (2006, 2014) GT is a 'constellation of methods'. For the purposes of this book it can be fundamentally understood as a methodology that contains various procedural guidelines, but with the caveat that these guidelines do vary greatly according to the school of thought and its associated authors. In fact, as the above-mentioned definition suggests, it can be considered in both ways: as a theoretical gaze on collection and analysis techniques ('a general method') and as some 'sets of procedures' and concrete tools for collecting and analysing data. I have used the plural here because, while as a method it does not make sense to speak of just one GT (there are varied instrumental approaches), there is only one methodology or methodological approach. The most important reminder for users of this approach is to always be well aware that these two levels coexist and be conscious of the level of abstraction in which they are positioning themselves.

3) *Systematically*. This attribute, added in brackets in the definition since it appears frequently in many other excerpts, emphasizes the functional aspects of the method. A peculiar trait of GT, that in the eyes of its proponents distinguished it from the very outset from the unsystematic impressionism of other qualitative approaches, was precisely the fact that its procedures are systematic in nature. In the 1960s, and even today, qualitative methods were considered to lack validity, and were even less reliable because they were highly conditioned by the impressionistic subjectivism of the researcher and by the lack of rigour characterizing their procedures. Qualitative research lacked the standardized procedures of quantitative research, and no alternatives were being proposed that allowed researchers to maintain certain essential features which, legitimately, the academic community expects from research findings: that the interpretations (or representations) coincide to a given degree to the reality under investigation, and that the findings are able to explain phenomena through systematically organized statements and even provide predictions about those phenomena. GT provides procedures which are systematic but flexible, a set of functional aspects that do not circumvent the requirement for rigour imposed by the academic community on empirical researchers.
4) *Generating theory*. The outcome of research conducted with GT is a theory – a rational, dense, articulated and systematic interpretation

that is capable of accounting for the reality being examined. Alternatively and less ambitiously, it produces a *conceptual framework* (Charmaz, 2006). In general, broad, extensive social science theories are the outcome of theoretical or speculative activity. Conversely, social scientific empirical research rarely produces comprehensive theories; rather, it limits itself to testing hypotheses or providing descriptions. GT originally ambitiously sought to generate complex and articulated theories similar in nature to those produced by the theorists of many disciplines, including early nineteenth-century sociology with its *grand theories*. The ambitious originality of GT consists in the attempt to offer an interpretative theory of the phenomena being examined, namely, the kind of product we would normally expect to be generated by the speculative work of a given discipline's theorists and not by the empirical work of field researchers. Obviously, if we were to further define the controversial concept of 'social theory', it would be necessary to distinguish it from the classical logic-formal definition of theory used in the social sciences, where theory is considered a set of organized statements and assertions, systematically connected to each other, which can be empirically tested when its statements are transformed into operationalized hypotheses. Kathy Charmaz has noted that different authors use diverse concepts of theory even within the grounded theorists' community (2014, pp. 227–34): concepts such as empirical generalization, process explanation, a theoretical comprehension or even a relationship between variables.

A neat distinction between theory and empirical research developed over the course of the last century together with the positivist paradigm in the human and social sciences. The ambitious aim of constructing comprehensive theories disappeared from empirical studies, and the activity of theoretical production was, from some points of view, reduced to testing hypotheses obtained hypothetically or deductively from pre-existing theories. As a matter of fact, the creative work of theoretical formulation withered away in the very act of developing a hypothesis on the basis of a critical review of previous studies or the will to replicate preceding studies by modifying minor conditions. GT, instead, puts a great deal of stress on the close link between theoretical and empirical research and positions itself in the narrow space that welds or binds theory and empirical reality together.

5) *Grounded in the data.* However, the specific characteristic of the theory produced using this approach is that such theory has a clear empirical basis; that is to say, it is obtained *beginning from the data.* In some ways this might represent an oxymoron to some people, a contradiction in terms: a theory cannot be empirically grounded, and empirical exploration cannot lead to speculative theory. The founders make a clear distinction between armchair theory and the outcome of fieldwork. It is here that they introduce the concept, untranslatable in many other languages, of *grounded.* This term encompasses several meanings at the same time: rooted, based on, but also stranded (ships), grounded (aircrafts), laying the basis for, to instruct or educate in, to teach the basic rudiments of, to prepare a base drawing. There is thus something carnal or material in the grounding in the data of a GT; it is a vital foundation of the living experience of facts – strong, intense and sometimes even violent. At the same time, however, it is a precise, detailed rooting which, by virtue of that fact, can form the basis for subsequent constructions, a terrain on which to build complex formal theories. This type of theory is not only based on the facts or empirically obtained from the data but also something more: it conveys the meaning of an accurate, profound, vital rooting in lived experience. This trait imbues the GT approach and the type of theory it is able to produce with originality: a theory not dissimilar from that produced by theorists or philosophers but one constructed starting from an empirical investigation and, by its very nature, deeply anchored in the data. This *grounded* nature of the theory, its lived rooting in the womb of reality, is therefore the quality that then grants the produced theory a very marked practical-operational significance and the potential to be useful for practical users.

In this sense, 'grounded theory' should be understood as both the name of the methodological approach and its outcome, process and product; through GT, researchers are able to produce theory that is grounded.

1.2 Characteristics of the Method

Although a multitude of interpretations and a variety of methods and procedures have been developed and circulated over the last fifty years, we can nevertheless identify some relatively constant methodological traits that represent the fundamental characteristics according to which research studies can be defined as GT.

Indeed, as is often the case in qualitative research, the flexibility of methods and of tools – so important for effectively describing and interpreting complex phenomena that cannot be contained within the rigid boxes of other more standardized and strict methods – also gives rise to methodological confusion and inappropriate mixtures of structurally different methods. The tendency to engage in *method slurring* (Baker, West & Stern, 1992) undermines the specific traits of an approach, thus losing the researcher the chance to use it appropriately and coherently with the phenomenon being studied. Obviously, the very idea of science that underlies various qualitative approaches is not compatible with the pursuit of methodological 'purity', and it is likewise wholly legitimate to use, with caution and competence, mixed or multiple methods (Creswell & Clark, 2007; Morse & Niehaus, 2009). Nevertheless, in order to both 'transgress' the orthodoxy of a given method and use it in combination with others, it is important to thoroughly understand the specific nature of that method and be able to fully master its procedures.

Since misconception too often reigns supreme in concrete uses of GT, it can be said that when *any* of these characteristics, in whatever specific version, are missing, the researcher is not using GT. In fact, it is all too easy to fall into the trap of generally calling every generic inductive qualitative analysis GT (Hood, 2007). Unlike generic inductive models, GT provides a specific and systematic set of procedures. Moreover, there is a widespread tendency to use different GT approaches because researchers need to ground their qualitative analyses in a legitimating technical language. Barney Glaser complained that the great success of GT can be seen as due to the success of its recognized and authorized technical language – a 'legitimizing jargon' which, according to Glaser, may prevail over the substantial use of the method (Glaser, 2009).

It is for this reason that, even while maintaining the necessary flexibility and accepting a plural notion of GT encompassing a multiplicity of approaches and orientations, we must nevertheless recall the defining and distinctive traits of this approach that cannot be missing in any way, no matter what the user's preferred orientation may be (Glaser & Strauss, 1967; Charmaz, 2000, 2006, 2014). These traits are as follows:

a) *To generate a theory* or a conceptual framework. As discussed earlier, GT is a methodology that aims to inductively generate conceptual abstraction on the basis of empirical data. Applying analytical procedures associated with GT but not aimed at conceptual construction is absolutely legitimate; however, it cannot be called GT. In the next section (1.3), I will come back on the specific nature of the emerging theory in GT.

b) *To explore a process.* A process can be defined as the conceptual formulation of temporal sequences that connect individual events to each other by identifying the markers of their beginnings, ends and intermediate passages or stages (Charmaz, 2014, p. 344). It is certainly a key GT feature to explore a process and the key categories through which it organizes and to identify its stages and phases. Many qualitative methods, especially after the 'interpretative turn' in the social sciences, are analytically focused only or mainly on *language* or exclusively on *meanings*. The distinctiveness of GT is that, although it departs from language and meanings, it *searches for regularities* of conceptual type among the phenomena being analysed. In this sense, GT has the specific, unique trait of being particularly suited for the exploration not of static phenomena, but of the processes underlying those phenomena and their dynamics, understood in context.

   In contrast to many other approaches, the research questions that GT is able to answer relate to processes and complex actions. GT aims at bringing out the processes – social, psychological, educational and so on – underlying the phenomena being investigated. I will return to this point in more detail and by providing practical examples in Chapter 4 when talking about the formulation of the research question.

c) *To employ theoretical sampling.* Another hallmark of GT is a particular type of sampling or strategy for selecting units of analysis. Theoretical sampling is a procedure typical of GT and constitutively connected to its analytical premises and procedures; although this procedure has subsequently been used by other qualitative methods as well, it represents in itself a rigorous way of resolving the longstanding problem of sampling design, validity and reliability in qualitative research. This type of sampling is based on completely different assumptions from those of probabilistic sampling designed on a statistical basis. It does not refer to the range of the number of participants in relation to the overall population universe, seeking statistical representativeness. The very logic of theoretical sampling is completely different and is analytical by nature. It is a function of the analytical process and takes the form of a progressive extension, during analysis, of the number of the participants' characteristics. This extension is thus guided by the requirements of the work of theoretical conceptualization. In other words, the sample is not formed *a priori*, but rather during the research, by following up on the lacunae of the emerging theory. Namely, as the categories emerge and hypotheses are formulated, in order to 'saturate' (see Chapter 5, section 5.2.1.) the categories, it is necessary to gather further data from among subjects and contexts that exhibit precisely those characteristics on which the emerging theory is still weak.

In Chapter 5 we will discuss the logic of the functioning of theoretical sampling in more detail.

d) *To collect data and analyse them simultaneously.* Theoretical sampling is possible only on the condition that data collection and analysis occur simultaneously. Otherwise, it would not be possible to distribute the choice of participants over the entire course of the research, and the work of construction of theory would not be able to develop as it does, from the descriptive level to levels of ever-increasing conceptual abstraction.

Therefore, a researcher, like I described in the foreword, who first collects large amounts of data (as often happens in qualitative research) and then – having left the field and sat down in front of piles of transcriptions – goes on to address the issue of how to analyse this material, is not conducting GT, because GT instead requires collecting and analysing data at the same time. In addition to progressively expanding the sample, the work of coding, choosing the initial categories that are relevant for the research, reformulating the research question, defining the properties and attributes of the categories and delimiting the theory, all require periodic returns to the field for data collection guided by analytical reflection on the emerging categories. This is one of the most difficult aspects of doing GT, because preparing for data collection while keeping in mind the analytical dimension, and vice versa, is not only complex but also *counter-intuitive*, not necessarily something that comes naturally. Collecting and analysing data are extremely different mental procedures, and only lengthy training prepares a person to conduct them concurrently. It is almost like the fledgling pianist who has a great deal of trouble moving his or her right and left hands independent of each other, but who with practice can do it effortlessly.

I will come back to this topic in Chapter 5 when describing the operational steps of the GT development process in detail.

e) *To use the method of constant comparison at every level of analysis.* The method of constant comparison lies at the very heart of GT, so much so that it serves to identify the method itself. Indeed, from the beginning, constant comparison seemed to be the name for defining the method as a whole: two years before the release of the seminal volume *The Discovery of Grounded Theory*, an article by Barney Glaser entitled 'The Constant Comparative Method of Qualitative Analysis' appeared in the journal *Social Problems* (Glaser, 1965) and later was republished as chapter 5 of *The Discovery of Grounded Theory*.

Constant comparison is a general method of investigation in which data, labels generated from initial coding, different events observed, categories (compared among each other and with the data) and the properties of categories are constantly compared. In addition, the different interpretive perspectives of research team members or the use of different translations when working in cross-cultural contexts (Tarozzi, 2014, 2019) or even the comparison of emerged analytical categories and scientific literature represent further levels of constant comparison. The act of comparing elements that are different and even quite dissimilar is what paves the way for intuition, the driving force behind theory construction. Such a process is reminiscent of the operating mechanism of metaphors which, by linking highly distinct concepts, produce inferences, trigger insights and generate new knowledge at a higher conceptual level (Chapter 6, section 6.5). Constant comparison calls for continuously asking questions about the data at various levels of analysis, and these questions, by seeking out nexuses among data and concepts, help researchers to progress in their conceptual understanding of the phenomena under investigation.

f) *Research questions using sensitizing concepts.* Since GT aims to proceed, inductively, and construct a conceptual formulation starting from phenomena and events without the excessive use of pre-established interpretative categories, it has to devise research questions using relatively loose categories and definitions lest it inadvertently constricts the phenomena to be studied inside closed categories. For this reason, following the tradition of symbolic interactionism, it might be helpful to use what Herbert Blumer (1954, 1969) has defined as sensitizing concepts. Such concepts are soft and flexible rather than rigidly definitive; they are open to being more precisely defined through empirical work and not imposed *a priori* by the consolidated jargon of a certain discipline or field of study. For instance, terms such as 'agency' or 'bullying' or even 'special educational needs' are non-sensitizing concepts. If we were to use them in formulating our initial research question, they would impede the open and unprejudiced construction of GT analysis. More will be discussed on this topic in section 4.2.

g) *Conceptualization versus description.* At this point, it should be clear that GT leads to theory generation, and therefore the basic operation involved is *conceptualization* rather than *description* as required by most other methods. It is not necessary to dwell on this point any further here, suffice to note that all too often research studies claiming to use GT are actually unable to move beyond the descriptive level, however accurate, systematic and thorough it may be. Neophytes in particular tend, understandably enough, to be reluctant to allow enough space for intuition and instead remain closely tied to the data, participants' statements and direct observations of the contexts in question. In general, this would obviously be a valid approach, but GT requires that researchers instead depart from this empirical basis to leap ahead in terms of theorization, conceptualization and the formulation of information. Not everyone is capable of such an operation and certainly not always. However, a GT analysis that does not produce any form of modelling or conceptual construction of the process being analysed is not GT, even if it has duly employed all of the associated procedures and strategies.

   Conceptualization is a very difficult operation to carry out as part of the research practice, and Chapter 5 provides examples of how it takes shape at the various levels of coding and analysis.

h) *Production of memos and diagrams.* From a more formal and functional point of view, every GT analysis worthy of the name invariably involves some typical instrumental apparatus that meets the specific methodological needs of the method. First of all, there are *memos*. In this methodology writing notes on the research

> process, of a varying nature during the different stages of research, represents a meta-cognitive prop which is not just advisable, as in other approaches, but absolutely vital. It is here that theoretical construction occurs, here that the constant comparison is developed, here that theoretical sampling takes shape and here that the leaps of intuition and hypotheses that fuel the work can be made explicit.
>
> In these memos, the researcher writes the theoretical story of the analytical process, maps the approach he or she has carried out and identifies the directions to be pursued in the future. The analytical reflections written out here build the outline of the theory that will be systematically presented in the final report. They represent an extremely rich wealth of material that accompanies and stimulates theoretical production but does not leave any visible traces in the final product. The reflections in these memos serve as *scaffolding*, and just like scaffolds they are essential for accompanying and supporting the construction of a building but, once it has been completed, they are removed and forgotten about.

Diagrams work in a similar manner. They are not as common as memos, with the exception of situational analysis where they represent an essential methodological step (Clarke, 2005). Nevertheless, the inclusion of diagrams is a characteristic trait that often distinguishes an article or volume presenting a GT-based study. Indeed, conceptual maps, patterns, diagrams and illustrations sometimes also perform a *scaffolding* function at higher levels of theoretical elaboration, at which point they accompany the constant comparison of categories and macro categories that are already quite abstract. However, they are often included in final reports as well precisely due to their expressivity and potential ability to schematically summarize situations and processes that are difficult to summarize with language, especially the technical (and often colourless) language required by a scientific text.

At the beginning of Chapter 6, I will return to this topic, outlining types of memos and how they are actually used as part of the concrete research process.

1.3 The Specific Nature of the Emerging Theory

A theory can be understood as a systematic set of statements, the components of which are interconnected through explicit relationships that is capable of explaining phenomena and has a certain ability to predict. A theory can be empirically tested when its statements are expressed as operationalized hypotheses. As I have mentioned before, a theory understood in this way can also be detached from the data of any given empirical case. The so-called *grand theories* produced by the founding fathers of classical sociology are comprehensive but are not *grounded* theories.

On the other hand, as part of the process of transforming the social sciences into empirical sciences based on positivistic epistemology, it became necessary for researchers to obtain the findings of their investigative work empirically and disregard statements that could not be proven valid and rigorous through empirical testing. GT produces what can be defined as a *processual theory*, which explains and interprets a set of phenomena by highlighting their logical-temporal sequences and the key categories through which the set of phenomena organizes itself, in order to identify stages and phases (Charmaz, 2014). Thus, single events are studied not as static phenomena but rather as linked-up parts of a larger whole.

Although such a distinction has become outdated in many ways, Glaser and Strauss (1967) clearly set up an opposition between research aimed at *testing* theory and research they consider aimed at *producing* theory, which is in turn distinct from armchair theories. In other words, GT is different from the hypothetical-deductive method (sometimes called the hypothetico-deductive method) of research, and it proposes a method, also empirical, to rigorously produce a theory through an *inductive*, or more precisely *abductive*, approach (for a closer inspection of the concept of abduction, Chapter 6, section 6.5). On closer inspection, as we will see in the next chapter when dealing with recent developments in GT, following the interpretative turn in the social sciences, the inductive process seen as leading towards the 'discovery' of theory has been thoroughly questioned. According to this more recent view, theoretical construction is the outcome of more complex meaning negotiation processes involving participants, context and researcher. It can thus be said that a GT is not limited to collecting and analysing data to confirm or refute pre-existing theories devised elsewhere by someone else, but rather creatively and rigorously constructs a theory, starting from the data, with the capacity to explain the phenomena in question.

Glaser and Strauss highlighted three typical features of GT which distinguish it from other methods of empirical research. Specifically, a GT has to *fit* the data, be *relevant* and *work*. Glaser (1978) later added a fourth feature to these original three, that of *modifiability*. As these features define in an original way the type of theory that this approach can offer, it is worth delving into these features and their implications in more detail.

a) *It conforms to the data (fit)*. Every GT (as an outcome of research) needs to fit the data and correspond and conform to the data. This means that researchers should not force data to correspond to a pre-existing theory, or selectively choose only those data that conform to it; in GT, the interpretative categories have to match the data. Obviously, this principle does not apply only to GT. To be reliable, all research needs to meet this criterion. The specificity of GT in this respect lies in the fact that, when using this method, the fit between data and theory is not the result of an ethical choice or exercise of intellectual honesty on the part of the researcher who fairly neither ignores data that would contradict their categories nor (essentially the same thing) choose exclusively those data that do conform. In GT the categories are inductively grounded in the data, and thus the criteria of data-conformation or fitting is applied automatically. Any data that does not conform indicates that the categories are not sufficiently saturated, or that it is time for the researcher to extend and correct the research accordingly.
b) *It is relevant*. A GT analysis has to be relevant to the area of inquiry it refers to. This means that a theory produced using this method has to meet two criteria:

   - It has to have a high degree of analytical power
   - It has to be conceptually dense or powerful.

   Namely, it is not enough to produce a formally correct, empirically grounded and rigorous theory, the outcomes of which say little about the complexity of the investigated situation, merely conveying simple statements that might even have already been intuitively familiar to the people working in that area. Too often, research based on a hypothetical-deductive structure reduces the variables to be observed to those few ones that can be isolated to control the research process, thus inevitably simplifying the complexity of the social context in question. However, qualitative research (for instance, conversation analysis) also quite often focuses on micro phenomena by isolating them to produce analyses that are rigorous and extremely thorough but which lose the ability to explain and make the broader phenomena comprehensible. Regarding the lack of conceptual density, many qualitative analyses may succeed in maintaining the complexity of the context being observed (for instance, an ethnography) but nonetheless produce descriptive outcomes that are conceptually flat and devoid of that theoretical thickness and richness that makes an inquiry relevant and meaningful. Stopping at the descriptive level, they fail to engage in abduction and end up lacking depth, simply repeating the research question in other words. While this is acceptable for some qualitative methodologies, GT is expected to do something different; it is expected to say something previously unknown. Unfortunately, too often GTs are procedurally sound and rigorous but fail to say anything. Relevance in terms of both explicative power and conceptual density is instead a typical feature of the theory produced with this approach, in contrast to that produced by other research traditions.

c) *It works*. The high explanatory capacity and conceptual density are features of GT that make the theory potentially useful, in a practical sense, to people working in the field. A theory that is *grounded* cannot ignore the needs of practitioners; it is required to produce outcomes that are meaningfully relevant and thus applicable. The practical value of the theory does not stem from researchers' particular sensitivity to the needs of practical users. Rather, it is useful because 'working' really is an essential feature of a theory produced in accordance with this approach. A GT analysis *works* because it really explains, fully and systematically, what takes place in a certain substantive area, and its outcomes are clear and, especially, can be transformed into decision-making processes which are comprehensible to practical users, those working in the area under investigation.

In education, as in many other practical areas, research cannot stop at description alone. Participants, rightly enough, request that there is practical value in it for them. They pose a thoroughly fair 'so what?' question to researchers, and the latter are challenged to deal with this request in a methodologically sound fashion. If categories fit, and if theory is meaningful and relevant, then practitioners and lay people can recognize themselves in the results, and these results will fit the contexts within which they were generated.

Too often, research (even qualitative research) instead stops at the descriptive level, offering a representation of the investigated reality that may well be scientifically correct and accurate, but is actually devoid of any use value for professionals or policymakers and thus may fail to meet their expectations. The fact that it works is certainly the main reason why GT has spread in particular among those disciplines where research requires not only rigorous and accurate investigations, but outcomes that are potentially useful for practical users and can be translated into practice. These constitutively practical disciplines – such as nursing, the sociology of health, organizational studies, information technology, marketing and education – have been the ones to successfully employ this method precisely due to the applicability of its outcomes. If the categories fit the data, and if the theory produced is relevant and says something meaningful about the contexts in question, then practical users will be able to engage with the outcomes and the language through which they are expressed, and these findings will be appropriate to the contexts in which they have been generated. This makes them useful and concrete; what is more important, it means they can easily be transformed into practices and transformative directions, such as a business reorganization or the definition of the training needs of professionals.

d) *Modifiability*. A theory that is *grounded* has the capacity to last over time, but it is a process in constant movement. No theory is fixed once and for all. The emergence of new data, new practical situations, and structural or historical changes leads a theory to be constantly modified even if the basic social process that constitutes the gist of the theory remains substantially unchanged. Unlike other experimental studies where hypotheses reformulation is an extremely conceptually cumbersome and financially costly process, in GT it is quite easy to modify your categories and the relationships among them as well as to add new categories in light of new, unexpected data. However, modifying an interpretative theory does not invalidate or refute the research or make it outdated. The ability of a theory to be modified emphasizes its dynamic and processual character; the theory is not disproved by the emergence of new

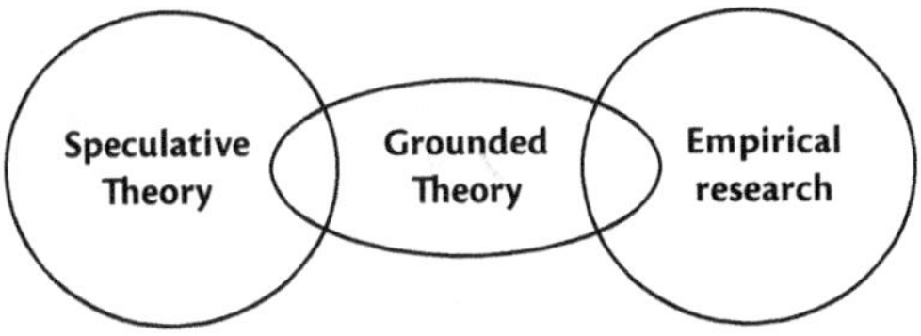

Fit	×	✓	✓
Relevance	✓	✓	×
Utility	n.a.	✓	n.a.
Modifiability	n.a.	✓	n.a.

Figure 1 GT's peculiar profile between theoretical-speculative and empirical research.

and unexpected data, but rather requires further development in the direction indicated by the newly emerged data. Therefore, an emerging theory may last quite a long time, but it requires periodic maintenance work in order to continue *fitting* data that might change over time or to be applicable to other contexts not previously considered.

These characteristics add up to a quite specific portrait of the theory produced with the GT method, a portrait which distinguishes it, on one hand, from the theoretical-speculative activity that generates a theory in a non-empirical manner (which does not conform to data and is not always relevant for professionals, practitioners and policymakers) and, on the other hand, from empirical research activity that allows little room for theoretical formulation (limiting itself to mainly testing or specifying the theory), which of course fits the data but is scarcely relevant and of little or no practical use (Figure 1).

1.4 Epistemological Assumptions

The earlier texts of GT do not dwell on outlining the epistemological background into which the new theory fits. This is partly due to a pragmatic style that favours functional and procedural aspects without digressing too much into theoretical-philosophical speculation – a style that actually sometimes casts such speculation to be nothing but useless and misleading abstraction. Above all, however, GT is presented as a methodological approach that arises from research practice. After Glaser and Strauss's innovative field-based studies in hospital wards hosting terminally ill patients, studies that were quite successful among sociologists at the time, they were asked to explain the research procedures they had used but left largely implicit in the text *Awareness of Dying* (Glaser and Strauss, 1965).

The earlier GT texts in particular do not explicitly lay out the epistemological elements that would identify the specific research philosophies this methodology is indebted to. Nevertheless, although it is outside the scope of this book to discuss the theoretical issues underlying the research in detail, a few brief considerations on the theoretical bases of GT are necessary. Interested readers are encouraged to refer to the more in-depth discussions in other texts (Charmaz, 2000; Strübing, 2007 and Bryant, 2009, among others).

Personally, I disagree with those who argue that GT should be regarded as a neutral tool regardless of the epistemology in which it is rooted because it does not fit any established research paradigm (Holton, 2007; Holton & Walsh, 2017). On closer inspection, the lack of any explicit reference to epistemology can represent a limitation. Indeed, it has historically limited GT in that, lacking any specific reference epistemology, over time GT has been the target of endless debates among the advocates of different approaches based on different research paradigms: positivist, constructivist, pragmatism and symbolic interactionism. This prolonged debate has led to a progressive 'erosion' (Greckhamer & Koro-Ljunberg, 2005) in the distinctiveness of the method.

Nevertheless, although the epistemological antecedents of GT are not always made clearly explicit in early texts, some such antecedents can be identified. In particular, we can identify the main theoretical currents in certain research philosophies on which this methodology has drawn.

In the first instance, as we will see in more detail in the next chapter, GT's theoretical references can be said to be closely linked to the two founders' different backgrounds and the theoretic-methodological directions they pursued. On the one hand, there is the tradition of analytical rigour in keeping with a positivistic style which characterized the sociological approach of Columbia University school where Barney Glaser studied; on the other hand, there is the pragmatist tradition tied to the field research of the Chicago school where Anselm Strauss studied.

In brief, we can identify three epistemological premises; a fourth one can also be added, one which does not represent a direct antecedent, but I will argue that this could constitute a theoretical reference point and a solid and contemporary epistemological background.

1) A *quantitative sociological paradigm* that owes much to Paul Lazarsfeld, Glaser's teacher at Columbia and one of the originators of an empirical sociology rooted in statistics. This paradigm makes its mark on GT through the so-called classic approach of ontological realism and epistemological objectivism, positions from which GT writers have been painstakingly trying to free themselves of late.

   The idea of 'discovering' a theory, the systematic formalization of the methods and procedures, the idea of rigour and the explicit reference in GT to quantitative and statistical methods stem from this epistemological genealogy.
2) The philosophy of *pragmatism* that so profoundly influenced the sociological school of Chicago and its pioneering, proto-ethnographic field study from the 1920s onwards (Park & Burgess, 1921). The influence of pragmatism is mainly indirect, filtered through the innovative methodologies of the Chicago school and its impact on symbolic interactionism. However, the nexus between theory and praxis and statements regarding the power of intervention and transformation of praxes into theory make explicit reference to the philosophy of John Dewey, one of the few philosophers explicitly mentioned by Glaser and Strauss in their founding text. A number of scholars have recently highlighted the close ties between GT, especially in the work of Anselm Strauss, and the tradition of early pragmatism (Mead, Dewey, Peirce) (Strübing, 2007; Bryant, 2009, 2017; Thornberg, 2012), and even Kathy Charmaz (2005) suggests links with the Chicago school – its pragmatist tradition and symbolic interaction – be renewed.
3) *Symbolic interactionism* appears to be GT's first theoretical framework of reference in the context of early pragmatism even though Glaser explicitly rejected the idea in a conversation with me (Glaser & Tarozzi, 2007). Symbolic interactionism has been changed transformed in particular through the teaching of Robert Herbert Blumer (1954), whose early work is quoted extensively in *The Discovery of GT*. Blumer's assumption is that human beings are symbolic animals who produce their own culture and interpret their own history through symbolic

systems (Mead, 2015/1934). This explains the focus on processes of ascribing meaning in the idea and practice of research. Social and psychosocial analysis focuses on the processes through which subjects grant meaning to the world they live in. However, ascribing meaning to the world is not an individual process, a mere product of consciousness; rather, it always takes place through interactions among subjects. It thus follows that society, the social reality, and even the idea of self are socially constructed through interaction, and this explains why the analysis of language takes on such a central place in the research inspired by this theoretical approach. It is in language that individual and social meanings are constructed and that these manifest through action. Another typical element of symbolic interactionism is its focus on the processes underlying the networks of meaning that characterizes the social world. The heuristic focus is not on static phenomena, but on their constant becoming, processes of transformation, the mechanisms (always built through interaction, never rigid or structural) that govern development and change. Hence, a theme that owes a great deal to the sociology of Simmel and seems to be so central to GT, symbolic interactionism looks for the invariable elements, the forms of social life that underlie the networks of meaning, processes of change and interactions among subjects. The idea that research can lead to identifying the basic social process underlying phenomena and that a general (formal) theory can then be developed capable of integrating various local (substantive) theories linked to specific contexts are based in part on symbolic interactionism. Glaser and Strauss's volume *Status passage* is strongly influenced by the theoretical approach of symbolic interactionism when it seeks to establish an overall, formal theory of social status change in various empirical situations by finding a common interpretative theory in contexts that are very different from each other and by developing a number of transversal categories that have meaning for all of the contexts of status transition considered by the researchers (Glaser & Strauss, 1971).

1.4.1 Phenomenology as Philosophy of Research

Phenomenology might be considered a direct albeit very remote or an indirect antecedent of GT, but under certain conditions it can constitute a true epistemological background or, more accurately, a research philosophy for this approach. Connecting phenomenology and GT can be regarded as controversial, since as research methodologies they are rooted in different theoretical backgrounds and they aim at different epistemic goals. However, from a theoretical perspective, phenomenology might be argued to constitute a theoretical horizon with the capacity to ensure methodological rigour that represents an alternative to positivistic rigour. It does so mainly by providing a clear theory of the experience that conforms well to the epistemic perspective of GT and, more generally, a way of thinking that is dense with the implications of practising this type of research.

On a methodological level, GT and phenomenology have traditionally been considered alternative and divergent approaches in empirical research (Baker et al., 1992).

Baker in particular highlights intellectual and methodological differences between GT and phenomenology, noting that this latter essentially aims to provide an inner (and therefore more psychological) description whereas GT aims at conceptualization (external and thus sociological).

Despite their differences, some scholars have tried to find commonalities between phenomenology and GT. Following in the footsteps of Ferente Marton (1986), Richardson (1999) in particular introduced the phenomenographic approach (in education) – an approach that is part of the phenomenological tradition but with methodological applications that explicitly refer to GT.

However, my argument is that the most significant similarities and complementarities between phenomenology and GT can be found at higher levels of conceptualization, and phenomenology can be regarded here as more of a philosophy of research than a methodology (Tarozzi & Mortari, 2010). Phenomenology cannot be considered a proper paradigm, but it is a theoretical framework, a world view, and a theoretical pillar for a scientific Kuhnian paradigm. In this sense, a focus on the nature of data and the knowledge coming from it is necessary. In recent decades, the second generation of grounded theorists (Charmaz, Bryant, Clarke) have focused on epistemological premises ignored by the GT initiators. Here I would like to highlight some ontological issues, inextricably interconnected with the epistemological underpinnings of GT. In particular, my argument draws from European phenomenology.

As a convenient philosophy of research, phenomenology could provide GT with a theory of knowledge and especially a theory of experience that is necessary to inform the methodology grounding its logic and analytical criteria but also and especially to clarify the epistemic nature of 'data'.

A phenomenological style of thinking can offer the researcher possible answers to ontological and epistemological questions. In particular, in phenomenology the ontological (*What is reality?*) is indistinguishable from the epistemological (*How do we know what we know?*). Ontological problems do not pertain exclusively to either metaphysical or positivistic perspectives and, according to a recent Husserlian interpretation (De Monticelli, 2007), phenomenology *is* an ontology. Phenomenology is ontologically revolutionary as far as the relationship between appearance and reality is concerned, and this is a key point for researchers with a number of consequences in terms of their theoretical understanding of what constitutes data in empirical research. In particular, according to Husserl's Göttingen circle, a phenomenological ontology accepts the existence of things outside of the mind that thinks about them. It is thus a somewhat realist ontology but differs from an objectivist epistemology (Guba & Lincoln, 1994) in that this latter instead conceives reality as a faithful mirror of the objective order of things. Phenomenology allows researchers to take on the social world and the things in it as existing outside of our consciousness, but this does not imply that the meanings of these things exist independently of our consciousness.

Thanks to its moderate realism, phenomenology provides empirical research with a theory of experience. Many qualitative methodologies including GT need a theory of experience that offers an ontological background, one which can make sense of the idea of data, sample, description and coding, and can handle all of these concepts critically. This is especially true of GT given that, as rightly stressed by Kathy Charmaz, there have been some significant ambiguities in its application precisely because it fails to take the epistemological question into account (Charmaz, 2000).

'The external world' is a big problem, a thorny challenge for all qualitative researchers but particularly for those who conduct research in highly practical fields such as education or nursing and must produce results which are useful to practitioners. This is the dilemma, and at time the anguish, of qualitative researchers as they seek lines of coherence, recurrences and rational structures within a reality which is itself complex. They cannot but be plagued by the awareness that any attempt to order such multidimensionality must absolutely avoid reductionism and oversimplification.

To take this ambiguity into account and live within this dilemma, researchers must not take the ontological and epistemological underpinnings of doing GT for granted.

For example, what does 'data' mean? What does it mean to 'collect' or 'gather' data? The term 'data' is the plural past participle of the Latin verb *dō* (to give). As such, it connotes something fixed, established or *given*. It alludes to a vision of reality coherent with positivistic assumptions in which the objects are *there*, in the world; it is thus quite distinct from the theoretical claims of qualitative research, where understanding subjects' meaning seems to be more important than collecting unbiased data. The verbs 'to collect' and 'to gather', referring to data, likewise encompass an act of epistemic investigation which includes assembling reality samples so that they can be objectively analysed by a neutral observer. Unsurprisingly, some scholars prefer to 'construct data' instead of 'collecting' them (Morse & Richards, 2002).

Without a proper ontology, related to an epistemology, GT cannot define the specific nature of the data collected and elaborated. For example, it cannot overcome the traditional impasse between data deriving from experience (and therefore directly observed by the researcher) and participants' personal accounts or formulations mediated by memory or subjective conceptualization through interviews.

GT researchers require ontological answers to these questions, a theory of experience consistent with this methodological choice. If they do not position themselves theoretically and critically, they tend instead to borrow natural scientific assumptions about reality, adopting what Husserl called a 'natural attitude'. Too often, both grounded theorists and other qualitative researchers embrace this naïve realism based on an epistemic attitude of mirroring knowledge not only out of epistemological laziness but also because of the evident advantages involved in adhering to the dominant scientific paradigm.

Unlike such a natural attitude, phenomenology offers an alternative theory of experience as a theoretical horizon in which GT researchers can find space for the various epistemic acts they have enacted. Data according to a phenomenological perspective is the experience of phenomena, the way in which consciousnesses make sense to their world. This conceptualization of experience is the description of the phenomenon as it appears to my consciousness. Objects, like the research data summarizing, representing and symbolizing them, do not live in the mind; they are not mental events, as extreme subjectivism or scepticism would seem to suggest. Nor are they 'things' that objectively exist in the world, however (or, at least, I have legitimate doubts about this). What they are is phenomena offering themselves to our consciousness. They are tracks, signs that allow us to describe (or intuit) opinions, perceptions, circumstances, symbols, representations, visions and so on.

In this sense, a phenomenological perspective invites GT researchers to take what they see seriously. It is a philosophy of attention, of an approach carefully describing the visible contours of things but following their hidden shapes. This quality makes phenomenology quite distinct from relativism, subjectivism or scepticism in terms of knowledge. Visible phenomena are not subjective projections of my perception but rather entities to reckon with, and the same can be said for social phenomena. Phenomenology, as a method aimed at researching knowledge rigorously, presupposes the existence of a phenomenon to which we can be faithful. Fidelity to the phenomenon is the 'principle of principles', as Husserl states in *Ideas I* (Husserl, 1913/1982).

According to Husserl, this is the 'realism' of phenomenology. A realism which is intersubjective, not objectivistic, and based on the principle of fidelity to the phenomenon that is extremely significant for social research. As such, it can also offer GT the theory of experience it needs.

The project of building the ontology of the real that is essential to GT could be underpinned by the theory of experience provided by Husserlian phenomenology. This viewpoint delineates a 'third way' positioned between two opposite extremes: a neo-positivist objectivism that a-critically assumes the existence of objects in the world and believes it is possible to discover the universal laws that govern these objects, and a radical postmodern subjectivism, sceptical and relativistic, that denies the very possibility of rigorously thinking about the world and thereby thwarts any attempt to investigate phenomena in any sense other than their discursive construction.

To Sum Up

This chapter has explored the essence of the specific nature of GT, which can be understood as both a research method and a methodology, on multiple, parallel levels:

- It analytically dissects a general definition of GT, and its elements have been unpacked one by one.
- It presents the characteristics of the method, those real 'hallmarks' that make the approach original in terms of its operational procedures and the methodological assumptions underpinning them.
- It suggests that GT constitutes the link between the speculative approaches of theoretical production and rigorous empirical research. Thanks to its position in this middle ground, at the highest level, GT has four characteristics that represent the strengths and weaknesses of the two furthest ends of the continuum: conforming to the data, being relevant, 'working' effectively, and remaining open to changes over time.
- It mentions the methodological prerequisites of GT, which are not always explained well in seminal GT texts. It identifies three theoretical reference points; namely, the quantitative sociological paradigm, pragmatism and symbolic interactionism, and also adds the fourth one of phenomenology while, however, arguing that this latter can only indirectly represent an epistemological antecedent.

Further Readings

On the Characteristics and Key Elements of GT

Birks, M., & Mills, J. E. (2012). *Grounded Theory: A Practical Guide*, 2nd edn. Los Angeles: Sage, chap. 4.

Charmaz, K. (2014). *Constructing Grounded Theory: A Practical Guide through Qualitative Analysis*, 2nd edn. London: Sage, Chap. 1.

Dey, I. (1999). *Grounding Grounded Theory: Guidelines for Qualitative Inquiry*. San Diego: Academic Press.

Flick, U. (2018). *Doing Grounded Theory*. Los Angeles: Sage, Chapters 1 and 2.

Glaser, B. (1998). *Doing Grounded Theory: Issues and Discussions*. Mill Valley, CA: Sociology Press.

Glaser, B. G., & Strauss, A. L. (1967). *The Discovery of Grounded Theory: Strategies for Qualitative Research*. Chicago: Aldine de Gruyter.

2 Historical Context

2.1 The Origins: A Small Sociological Revolution

When it was published, Glaser and Strauss's book, dedicated to studying the awareness of dying in the contexts of Californian hospitals (Glaser & Strauss, 1965), was an enormous success both nationally and internationally. This pioneering work, still at least somewhat relevant even today, impressed experts and professionals by the depth of its analysis and rare ability to develop a comprehensive theory about a topic that had yet to be fully investigated, especially with qualitative tools. The content and method of the research, as well as the creative connections between these two dimensions, confirmed its innovative character. In medical sociology, it was innovative to address the theme of the awareness of dying in the hospital with all its social, psychological and even existential implications. Moreover, given the nature of the topic, consolidated sociological research methods such as surveys would have had trouble capturing the intensity, depth and gravity of the experience under investigation, however socially concealed and tendentially removed from daily practices it might be. To grasp the processes that dying triggered in hospitals required venturing into the field to gather dense, rich, in-depth data. Therefore, choosing a qualitative approach to this field represented a choice that was innovative but, at the same time, necessary to adequately deal with the theme of death in this context.

Anselm Strauss had moved to San Francisco in 1960 where he established the Department of Social and Behavioural Sciences as a development of the first doctoral programme for nurses within the School of Nursing in the University of California. Twenty years younger than Strauss, Barney Glaser was born and raised in San Francisco, and after two years spent in Europe, received his PhD from the Columbia University in New York. He was invited by Strauss to join the study on the dying as research scientist. According to Stern (2009), the two had met 'at a gathering' a few years before and Glaser was aware of the theoretical work of his senior partner.

The research team run by Glaser and Strauss[1] conducted a set of observations in various wards of multiple hospitals, mainly in California but also at some hospitals abroad, in which the dynamics of an awareness of dying were evident. In these sites, they carried out in-depth interviews and long informal conversations about the ways, timing and circumstances in and through which medical staff and terminal patients communicated the news of imminent death and how this was managed or concealed by the nursing staff, patients and families. They formulated an original theory which systematically accounted for the social organization and temporal structuring triggered by processes of dying and the ways this topic was communicated or omitted from conversational exchanges among doctors, nurses and patients.

The method was new. It had been created in the field to meet the specific requirements of a broad (but not reducible), difficult (but hard to simplify) and uncomfortable (but worth exploring) research question: What happens in hospital settings when a patient is about to die? This research question was explored by Glaser and Strauss throughout four books, and these also became the four founding texts (Bryant & Charmaz, 2007) describing an innovative methodological approach.[2]

The immediate success and scientific recognition enjoyed by that first book granted new energy and courage to researchers who, conducting qualitative research on a daily basis, grappled with the frustration of not having the fruits of their work acknowledged; rather, the mainstreaming scientific community considered such research to be impressionistic, subjective and therefore essentially unscientific.

Given this context, many colleagues insistently asked the two San Francisco-based sociologists to outline the methodological details of the approach they had followed to conduct the research, to demonstrate the rigour of their conclusions to a sceptical academic community of sociologists and, especially, to legitimate the subsequent work of numerous other qualitative researchers. *The Discovery of Grounded Theory* was the answer to this growing demand (Glaser, 1998). To comprehend the reasons behind qualitative researchers' urgent search for legitimation at that time

[1] Glaser and Strauss were joined by Jeanne Quint Benoliel, a professional nurse whose important role was largely neglected in this research (Bryant, 2017; Stern, 2012).

[2] *Awareness of dying* (1965), *The Discovery of grounded theory* (1967), *Time for dying* (1968) and *Status passage* (1971).

as well as the innovative power of GT as an answer, it is necessary to return, albeit briefly, to the climate characterizing the social science departments of American universities during the Sixties.

At that time, the thinking and teaching of social research methodology referred exclusively to quantitative and statistical research. Talking about research methodology meant talking about statistics. It is not that qualitative research was lacking. The Chicago school of Robert Park and Ernest Burgess (Park & Burgess, 1921) had been active since the end of the first decade of the century and had produced a great deal of field-based qualitative studies but, although sociologists continued to carry out qualitative research in the following decades, there was no serious and rigorous set of manuals to formalize qualitative procedures (Gobo, 2005). It is this lacuna that led Giampietro Gobo to observe that *The Discovery of Grounded Theory* with its eloquent subtitle *Strategies for Qualitative Research* is 'commonly recognized as the first contribution articulated on qualitative methodology' (Gobo, 2005, p. 69).

In hindsight, it can be argued that part of the success of this book is due to the particular historic circumstances in which it came to light. This first text on qualitative research methodology was issued precisely at a moment plagued by a crisis of legitimation of qualitative approaches and in what might have been the most fertile season for quantitative methodologies within the social sciences. The success of the book (and the methodology) came about quite slowly, however. Barney Glaser wrote thirty years later that their book was fifteen or twenty years ahead of its time (Glaser, 1998): *Discovery* did not go unnoticed, but its true success came later, when other scholars began to apply the method outlined in the book with success (Glaser & Tarozzi, 2007).

Towards the end of the 1960s, at the time of Glaser and Strauss's book, qualitative research was in a state of severe crisis, delegitimized and unrecognized due to both internal and, especially, external factors. Internal, stemming from the slightly anarchic, unsystematic and refractory tendency many qualitative researchers displayed in terms of formalizing their procedures. External, deriving from the dominant positivist paradigm's tendency to challenge the very scientific validity of qualitative methods. According to the narrative of prevailing social science in that period, researchers were to produce nomothetic (that is to say, capable of gathering and formulating universal laws) and generalizable outcomes based on statistically representative samples of the population under investigation.

These methods were taken to be reliable, and thus research conducted using the same methods and under the same conditions was expected to produce the same results. By transforming data into quantifiable measures, social scientists were able to subject the data to statistical processing and thereby guarantee the indisputable scientific validity of the results.

With this dominant idea of scientific knowledge, there was little room for research that privileged depth over breadth, significance over reliability and theory building over the experimental verification of hypotheses. Such research was simply outside the comfort zone of sociology as a 'normal science' (Kuhn, 1996/1962) busy applying the prevailing scientific paradigm; it was excluded by the scientific community that identified with and was legitimized by this same paradigm. The main reason the social scientific community tended to exclude qualitative approaches was that qualitative methods were not able to produce data analysis on the basis of analytical procedures at least as reliable and valid as the sophisticated mathematical processing of variables offered by quantitative research.

It was in this context that *Discovery*, as a qualitative research methodology text, openly challenged many of the assumptions of the positivist paradigm. In so doing, it also legitimized alternative methods of social research and systematic qualitative analysis. Previously, qualitative research accounts had dedicated little space to an explanation of *how* the authors dealt with the systematic analysis of huge amounts of data. Although such methods often followed rigorous criteria and procedures as well, these methods were not made explicit. Failing to follow systematic and formalized procedures, they appeared more like unsophisticated know-how than science. This craft knowledge was built through the experience of slow and patient immersions in the field or learnt under the guiding hands of teachers supervising their students' work. With *Discovery*, this previously oral and implicit tradition was formalized and made accessible to all for the first time.

In summary, Glaser and Strauss's *small sociological revolution* proceeded in two directions (Charmaz, 2000): (*a*) it challenged the predominant sociological paradigm and (*b*) it offered concrete alternative guidelines for research practice. Added to these two main directions were some of the innovative and peculiar characteristics of the method – the possibility to produce theory from empirical research and all the associated implications in terms of procedure – highlighted in the previous chapter, and it is easy to see the originality of the gauntlet thrown down by GT.

2.2 The Strauss and Glaser Divide

In 1991, a lively correspondence between Anselm Strauss and Barney Glaser suggests that their relationship was severely compromised (cit. in Glaser, 1992). Glaser stated that the publication, produced by Strauss together with Corbin, of *Basics of Qualitative Research* 'misconceives our conceptions on grounded theory to an extreme degree, even destructive degree' (ivi, p. 1) and even went so far as to request the volume be withdrawn.

What were the reasons for such a harsh disagreement? What were these upheavals generated by Strauss's book, so momentous that it (allegedly) 'destroyed the concept of GT itself?' Beyond personal and professional reasons for the conflict, which are not worth rehashing here, it is interesting to explore the theoretical-methodological reasons for the separation between the two co-founders. Indeed, over time this divergence has given rise to two different approaches or, in reality, two separate schools.

The reasons behind this divergence cannot be traced back to Glaser and Strauss's different academic training, or if so, only indirectly. As mentioned in the previous chapter, GT lies at the confluence of two of the most important American sociological traditions of the twentieth century. One was the Chicago school with its tradition of qualitative field studies influenced by pragmatism. The other was the New York Columbia University realist school and teaching of the great quantitative methodologist Paul Lazarsfeld. Especially in the Chicago school, this confluence was further enriched by the influence of symbolic interactionism and its view of reality as a symbolic construction. In empirical research, this view translated into focusing on interactions and the meaning of daily actions. On the one hand, therefore, there was the analytical rigour, rational need for methodical order and focus on defining procedures so as to perform the same work of methodological systematization in the qualitative field that Lazarsfeld had carried out in the quantitative field. On the other hand, there was work in the field, openness to experience, attention to symbolic apparatuses and the flexibility of research practices.

It was not the distance between the theoretical backgrounds of the two founders that triggered the dispute between Glaser and Strauss however, their divergence occurred on other grounds. The root cause was the 1990 publication of *Basics of Qualitative Research: Techniques and Procedures for*

Developing Grounded Theory, a two-person volume by Strauss and his young assistant, Juliet Corbin (Strauss & Corbin, 1990, 1998; Corbin & Strauss, 2015 IV ed.). This book, conceived to offer university students a practical manual for conducting GT, enjoyed and still enjoys enormous success. Each excerpt is described in an extremely accurate and technical manner by offering the readers all over the world a highly accessible handbook featuring clear procedures and guidelines.

Glaser judged the approach presented in this book so distant from GT as to merit its own name, 'full conceptual description'. He outlined essentially three main criticisms.

1. There was too much emphasis on the technical aspects of the method. Although this framing was the main reason for the book's success, it harnesses the heart of the method of constant comparison within procedures that prove excessively rigid. For instance, Glaser argued that technically detailing the various phases of codification, open then axial and eventually selective, by affixing the first labels then grouping them to identify categories and macro categories, is not only a tedious and fundamentally useless exercise but also a dangerous technicality that inhibits free comparison among concepts. According to Glaser, it is only through such comparison that insights about categories and properties can emerge, a process that relies on the analytical skills of the researcher and not artificial technical expedients (Glaser, 1992, p. 43).
2. Moreover, Strauss and Corbin significantly shifted the method towards the verification of hypotheses rather than towards theory generation. Indeed, in Glaser's view the area of inquiry should be approached using a very open research question: 'What's going on here?' This question is later specified during the course of the first data collections and analyses, but it can never be expressed in a single, clear proposition before accessing the data. The logic of this assertion is clear enough: a method aimed at developing a theory based on the data cannot be based on *a priori* theoretical statements which forge a focussed research question. For Strauss and Corbin, instead, the research question is always expressed as a focussed statement summarizing the specific question through which the researcher intends to interrogate the phenomenon under investigation; this question is fundamental for reducing the scope of

the research focus within the bounds of a manageable question and, therefore, within a concretely feasible project (Glaser, 1992, cap. 4; Strauss & Corbin, 1998, cap. 4).

3. Above all, however, Glaser's main critique, which encompasses the two previous ones, is that the techniques proposed by Strauss and Corbin force the analysis into pre-established categories, thus betraying one of the central and defining points characterizing the very essence of GT as a methodology. For instance, some tools are presented and defined *a priori* to facilitate the researcher's application of the method in phases of more theoretical coding (which Strauss and Corbin call axial and selective coding), where the work of conceptualization becomes more sophisticated and complex. These tools help the researcher to analytically define the features of the emerging interpretative categories. This effort to facilitate the concrete application of the method also serves to imprison data and categories inside rigid and preconceived frames, however. These frames or 'coding paradigms' take consequences, dimensions, subcategories and properties that should instead emerge from the data and cast them as conditions. The result is a method, described in detail, which allows researchers to comb the data looking for the empirical evidence that would confirm (or, rarely, falsify) the starting hypothesis already implicit in the research question. This method does not allow users to remain open to the data; however, it allows them to listen to the data and to reveal what they will.

Besides these main initial reasons for divergence, over time the two authors also developed different approaches providing different interpretations of the notions presented in the founding text (theoretical sampling, coding, process, core category, etc.) and giving different names to the specific procedural stages. Indeed, the approaches are different enough that today it makes sense to refer to a (Morse et al., 2009) *Glaserian 'classic' approach*, to GT whose operational procedures are outlined in *Doing Grounded Theory* of 1998, and to a *Straussian approach* (now only Corbin's, after Strauss's death in 1996), codified in its techniques and methodological tools in the above-mentioned bestseller (Strauss & Corbin, 1990) and in following editions (1998; 2007 then Corbin & Strauss, 2015). It should be noted, however, that Juliet Corbin noticeably shifted her interpretation of GT towards a clear constructivist position in the last edition.

2.3 Subsequent Lines of GT Development

From the 1990s onwards a new generation of grounded theorists developed, guided by key figures from the GT second generation (Morse et al., 2009) such as Kathy Charmaz, Phyllis Noerager Stern, Adele Clarke, Juliet Corbin, Barbara Bowers, Susan Leigh Star and Carolyn Wiener, among others, from the doctoral programme at UCSF.

Meanwhile, between the publication of *Discovery* and the establishment of the second generation towards the end of the last century, there was a momentous shift in the social sciences that the two founders, even beyond their specific disagreements, could certainly not have foreseen: the interpretative turn in the social sciences and postmodernist climate.

The rise of the interpretative and constructivist perspective seriously undermined the positivist paradigm in the social sciences. It asserted an ontology, an epistemology, a theory of knowledge, an idea of science that was wholly different from and an alternative to those expressed by positivist empiricism (Guba & Lincoln, 1994).

However, traditional GT had adopted such a rigorous structure that, by a paradoxical twist of fate, it was actually more in line with that same positivism it had helped call into question. In fact, both 'schools' of canonical GT display some positivist traits.

- *Realist ontology*. The very idea that a theory can be 'discovered' assumes a realistic view of the phenomena subject to investigation in which objects of knowledge exist in the world independently of the subjects who perceive them.
- *Objectivist epistemology*. The objects of reality can be known objectively through the use of suitable heuristic tools since they correspond to some objective reality.
- *Theory–reality* correspondence. The idea that then-expressible theories can be developed (complete with replicable methods) through rational models assumes twofold isomorphism, both between research data and investigated phenomena (governed by mechanical laws), and between these and the rational theory expressing them.
- *Separation between researchers and their object*. Researchers are discoverers who grasp the dynamics underlying visible phenomena.

They are able to control and reduce their own 'pollution' of the data and to produce a substantive or formal theory that corresponds to objective reality.
- *Generalizability*. The theories produced by researchers have elevated generalisability power because they have theoretically characterized a phenomenon in its objective nature and have identified its antecedents and causal nexus.

Although GT methodology cannot be reduced to entirely positivist approaches (and indeed, GT has expressly criticized such approaches), it is nevertheless affected by the paradigm prevailing at the historical moment it was developed. Since the 1990s, some representatives of the 'second generation of grounded theorists' have worked to profoundly question the paradigm underlying this view of scientific knowledge. An alternative view has been proposed in which the subject who knows (i.e. the researcher) is instead considered an active co-constructor of the reality instead of describing it objectively. The objectivity of scientific knowledge is not an attainable goal in social research, the only possible outcome are interpretations of the reality. At the close of the twentieth century, the crisis of modern rationality and rethinking of the epistemologies that accompanied the scientific revolutions of modernity gave rise to theoretical perspectives that seriously undermined consolidated paradigms. Viewed on a spectrum, such perspectives range from radical constructivism, that declares an end to any possibility of scientific thought together with the great narrations of the twentieth century, to more moderate positions that seek to re-establish new forms of scientific rigour for empirical research as an alternative to positivist rigour.

The new academic generation who have tried to rethink GT in light of the new perspectives in the social sciences is located in this space (Bryant, 2003). Examples include scholars such as Adele Clarke (2003, 2005) and especially Kathy Charmaz (2000, 2007), who has also focused on the practical applications of GT (Charmaz, 2006, 2014). It is worth introducing their approach, a development that has allowed scholars at the dawn of the third millennium to re-establish this methodology by attempting to free it from its few residual positivist traces while retrieving and reinvigorating its much more numerous innovative aspects.

Due to the fundamental role constructivist GT has played in liberating GT from its positivist remains and renovating and reviving it after the postmodern interpretive turn, it is worth explaining the original contribution of constructivist GT and the interrelated situational analysis approach in more depth.

2.4 Constructivist GT

Having acknowledged the positivist assumptions outlined earlier, Glaser's student Kathy Charmaz interpreted GT according to a constructivist perspective that (partially) accepts the idea of relativist knowledge somehow resulting from a multifaceted and plural conception of reality. Charmaz's contribution, following her research on chronic illness and its impact on patients' self-representation (Charmaz, 1973, 1991), is summarized in an enlightening article included in the second edition of the renowned *Handbook* edited by Denzin and Lincoln (2000), although many of these arguments had already appeared in an initial form in the special issue of *Qualitative Health Research* edited by Katharin May (1996) with a key contribution by Benoliel (see footnote 1) and Merilyn Annells.

Constructivist GT assumes that knowledge results from the mutual construction of the research on the part of both researcher and subjects, and thus the inquiry is based on the research data understood as *meanings* rather than facts. In particular, constructivist GT 'assumes a relativist epistemology, sees knowledge as socially produced, acknowledges multiple standpoints of both research participants and the grounded theorists and takes a reflective stance towards our actions, situations and participants in the field settings' (Charmaz, 2009, p. 129).

It is possible to have a constructivist GT that intentionally distances itself from its positivist traces as long as (*a*) it uses the procedural directions in a flexible manner and not as rigid requirements; (*b*) it puts the meanings that facilitate an interpretative comprehension at the centre of the analysis; (*c*) it uses the strategies proposed by the founders of GT without assuming their positivist assumptions (Charmaz, 2000).

Constructivist GT assumes that the researcher is not able to 'discover' a theory hidden in a reality understood as objective, and that this theory likewise does not constitute Truth with a capital *T*, with a generalizable character and unconditionally replicable procedures. Knowledge is instead the result of co-construction involving the researcher and subjects. Such a position entails some consequences for GT, consequences which are synthesized here, and the practical applications of which are covered in the following chapters.

- Researchers are inevitably part of the context that they observe. They do not presume to position themselves as neutral observers; rather, they assume their own viewpoint as research data even while trying to distinguish between data produced by observed facts and their own representations, perceptions and judgements.
- Data are not 'collected', they are in some way produced. Although the use of the term data 'collection' now prevails among researchers, this phrase immediately evoking the image of a researcher picking up objects sitting in front of them, constructivist GT refers to the 'construction' or 'generation' of data.
- The richest 'data' to be used are not 'facts' but primarily the *meanings* that specific subjects ascribe to those facts. In particular, researchers seek the tacit meanings attributed to facts, events and relationships – meanings the subjects themselves are not aware of but which guide their actions.
- The researcher's relationship with the subjects is particularly important (not just for ethical reasons), and 'data collection' tools must be well calibrated to these subjects and allow deep participation. The researcher is indistinguishable from the analytical mechanisms with which he or she formulates the meanings that emerged in the field. The work of negotiating meanings occurs not only during the generation of empirical data but also, on a different level, during the process of analysis. The interpretative dimension is always intertwined with descriptive and contextualizing processes.
- Such mechanisms must remain flexible, never rigid, to avoid corralling reality into grids produced by the analytical tools themselves. It is important to define categories flexibly and dynamically, avoiding denominations that close and objectivize in favour of terms which are relevant to the phenomena they express and which maintain consonance with the experience.
- The relationships among the categories developed by the researcher cannot be defined once and for all; they are always complex and multidimensional. Therefore, rather than identifying definitive casual links among them, it is preferable to develop the meanings attributed to them by the subjects and employed in various circumstances stemming from those categories.

- The final write-up is an integral part of the analysis, and the pursuit of clear, communicative and pleasant prose does not represent an unnecessary or, much less, anti-scientific limit. Instead, it constitutes a further area of theoretical construction.

Certainly, the constructivist perspective has also limitations. Some have highlighted that it is implicitly self-contradictory (Greckhamer & Koro-Ljungberg, 2005) for instance, or that it represents a mere declaration of principle without any coherent application of its practices. Indeed, it is not clear how a method that establishes detailed analytical steps a *priori* and provides particularized directions for conducting semi-structured interviews can truly be defined as constructivist. Certainly, such traits drastically reduce the space for the co-construction of data as opposed to actively involving participants in developing the meanings constructed through the exchange, as intended.

However, it must be noticed that Charmaz's GT constructivism is never a radical one. It does not embrace the most extreme assumptions of an anti-scientific postmodernism. Rather, Charmaz seems to advocate for soft relativism: 'My form of constructivism, however, does not subscribe to the radical subjectivism and individual reductionism assumed by some advocates of constructivism. In such analysis individual consciousness explains all' (Charmaz, 2009, p. 134).

A separate but closely related constructivist GT approach is that of *situational analysis*. Adele Clarke (2003, 2005; Clarke, Friese, & Washburn, 2018) coined this term to refer to a method of analysis she has outlined that develops and evolves GT in line with the postmodernist turn in the social sciences. A student of Strauss and a professor, now emerita, at the University of California in San Francisco's renowned department of social sciences, Clarke proposes a reshaping of GT within a post-structuralist and feminist frame of reference strongly influenced by an American reading of Foucault. *Situational analysis* further broadens the basis of usable data in a GT by including both the discursive practices that construct social reality and material data, the non-human. This latter is granted particular attention to give voice to the marginalized, those excluded from dominant social discourse.

It is especially in its analytical procedures that this approach reveals its remarkable innovative elements, however. Clarke proposes that traditional analysis be extended from the basic social process through the construction of increasingly complex analytical maps. In particular, she presents three types of map: situational, maps of social worlds and arenas, and maps of positionality along analytical axes.

This is a particular use of diagrams as an analytical tool (Chapter 6, section 6.2) to introduce themes and concepts and to generate conceptual order by defining various types of relationships. In this case, however, the order in question maintains the complexity of the phenomenon and does not reduce it to the mere social process: it also includes the pre-comprehensions of the researcher and uses conceptual maps to reveal the structural elements that limit and condition the situation being studied, such as individual, non-human, cultural, political, discursive, historical elements and so on. The result is a broader sociological frame, one that is perhaps less grounded in that the situational dimensions are indicated *a priori*, but which undoubtedly remains more open to macrosocial elements such as power, hegemony, discrimination and racism which are overlooked by classic GT, as well as non-neutral interpretive frameworks to look at data such as critical or feminist theories.

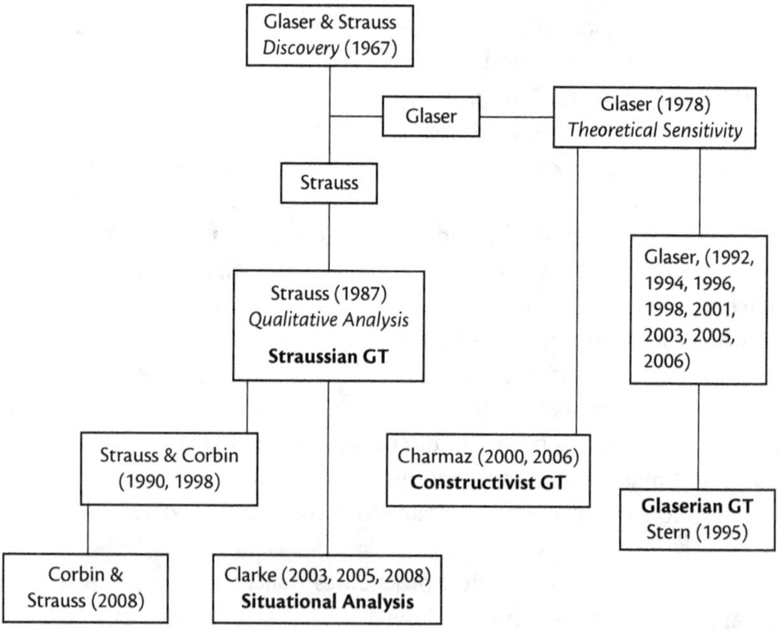

Figure 2 Genealogy of grounded theory.
Source: Adapted from Morse (2009).

In summary, in its fifty years of history GT has developed well beyond the intentions of its two originators by branching off into diverse perspectives. Following Glaser and Strauss's canonical positions, it has been argued that there are currently three major streams of GT, with the above-mentioned situational analysis constituting a fourth (Morse et al., 2009; Bryant, 2017).

The scheme (Figure 2) developed by Janice M. Morse, 2009, effectively summarizes the evolution of these broad streams of GT and their divergences in terms of methodological procedures, theoretical assumptions and philosophical orientations.

Table 1 briefly compares the three main current streams of GT.1

Table 1 Comparison of the Main GT Schools along Key GT Elements

	Classic GT	**Straussian GT**	**Constructivist GT**
Research question	Open. It is not a statement that identifies the problem to be studied. It is impossible to define in advance (one starts in an open manner from an area of investigation)	Focused. It is a statement that clearly identifies the problem to be studied. It allows the researcher to narrow the area of investigation and make it manageable	Sensitizing concepts. There is no statement. Sensitizing concepts launch the research
Type of data	'All is data'	Indifferent. Especially observations	Semi-structured interviews and textual analysis. Co-construction of data
Core category	It emerges almost magically to be suddenly grasped at the beginning or end of the research	To allow the *c.c.* to emerge requires intense manipulation of the data. There is not only one *c. c.*	There is a prevailing *c. c.*
Types of coding	Substantive Theoretical	Open Axial Selective	Initial Focused Axial Theoretical
Key textbooks	Glaser, 1978 Glaser, 1998 Stern & Porr, 2011 Holton & Walsh, 2017.	Strauss, 1987 Strauss & Corbin 1990; 1997; 1998 Corbin & Strauss 2008, 2015 Strauss & Corbin, 1997	Charmaz, 2000, 2006, 2014 Bryant, 2003, 2018 Clarke, 2003, 2005

These three approaches are not presented with the intention of establishing one as the most correct approach. The aim is instead to outline how the method has branched out over the last fifty years without indicating any form of birthright or establishing any methodological orthodoxy that users must comply with. In fact, although the approach presented in this volume is largely affected by the constructivist perspective, I agree with Kathy Charmaz's assertion (2006, p. 9) that GT is a set of principles and research practices that does not need to be taken as a *package* or as a specific provision to be followed meticulously. Users can instead treat it as an unsystematic and flexible set of procedural directions which must nevertheless be positioned within an original epistemological frame that distinguishes it from other qualitative methodologies without, however, any pretence of superiority.

2.5 GT Outside the United States

Notwithstanding the debate taking place entirely within the United States, or rather in the Bay area in northern California, since the beginning of this century and especially in the past decade, GT has been shaped by influences from outside the United States (Charmaz, 2014b). Beyond even the Anglo-Saxon world (Bryant, 2017 in the UK; Birks & Mills, 2012 in Australia), a substantial German tradition developed on the basis of the lectures Strauss gave in Germany in the 1990s (Kelle, 2007, Flick, 2018, Mey & Mruck, 2011) (see, for example, Hildenbrand, 2007; Reichertz, 2007; Schütze, 2008; Strübing, 2007), and GT has also evolved in northern (Thornberg, 2012), central (Konecki, 2011) and southern European countries (Tarozzi, 2008; Buscaglioni, 2013) as well as in Asia (Inaba & Kakai, 2019; Priya & Prakash, 2015).

This recent global expansion has contributed considerably to fuelling reflections on GT's theoretical foundations, largely ignored by the first theorists of GT, and on its relationship with other qualitative methods and research traditions.

2.6 Main Critiques

GT has been critiqued from different perspectives over the years (Dey, 1999; Thomas & James, 2006). And, as one might expect, in their presentations the various advocates of a particular approach have also critiqued each other's variants. Beyond such inter-differentiation, here is a summary of some of the main critiques levelled at the theory itself:

1. Some scholars (Silverman, 2000 among others) have called into question the very concept of theory underlying GT, arguing that it is not well defined or clarified, especially in the earliest works. Indeed, different grounded theorists' works present several different concepts of theory (Charmaz, 2006, p. 125), such as empirical generalization, process explanation, a theoretical comprehension or even a relationship between variables. Since GT is a qualitative methodology, this cannot be understood as a set of systematically organized statements capable of generating a hypothesis for empirical testing. However, GT is expected to result in a theory ex-post, therefore it does need to provide a definition of the theory, even processual theory, that we can legitimately expect as a research outcome (see previous chapter).
2. Other criticisms have been posed about the logic guiding the GT process (Dey, 1999; Kelle, 2005; Thornberg, 2012). In particular, it has been noted that this logic depends on inappropriate models of induction, and claims based on these models are therefore equally inappropriate for explanation and prediction (Thomas & James, 2006). Much has been written about the logic underlying the analytical process of GT and the concept of induction or abduction (Reichertz, 2010), an element which was largely taken for granted by the method's founding fathers.
3. GT has also been criticized for focusing on individuals and producing decontextualized analyses (Burawoy, 1991) that neglect social context and are therefore unable to investigate issues such as inequality, racism, oppression, hegemony and so on essential for a critical reading of society. This is particularly evident in the original GT (McDonald, 2001), but critics have argued that symbolic interactionism (Denzin, 1992) and radical constructivism that focussed solely on subjects' worldviews also suffer from this weakness. Kathy Charmaz has addressed this need for a GT committed to social justice and which also includes social circumstances in various presentations (Charmaz, 2005, 2014) and it has been at the centre of follow-up discussion at seminars and conferences.

4. Finally, as is the case with many research approaches developed in North America and the Anglo-Saxon world more generally starting from the twenty-first century, GT's spread far beyond the North American context in which it originated has been accompanied by critiques of the Anglo-centric character of qualitative research in general and GT in particular (Mruck, Puebla, & Faux, 2005; Cisneros Puebla et al., 2006; Hsiung, 2012). These critical stances have questioned both the dominance of the Anglo-American core and the current divide between qualitative research in the core and in the periphery. Arguing against this coloniality of knowledge, some critics have asserted the need for a post-colonial GT and measures to preserve local languages from the hegemony of English (Tarozzi, 2019).

Ultimately, as much as constructivist GT has tried to re-establish its underlying assumptions by separating them from their positivist residue, this methodology will always be incompatible with the paradigms of radical constructivism, on the one hand, according to which there exist only interpretations and not facts, and with neo-positivist paradigms, on the other hand, according to which there exist only facts and not interpretations.

To Sum Up

- Referencing the historical context in which GT was originated is useful for comprehending both the reasons for the (however delayed) success of the method and the sense of innovation it injected into methodologies of inquiry within the social sciences.
- GT challenged the dominant positivist paradigm from the outset, but it nonetheless remains caught up in some of its assumptions. The interpretative turn of the 1980s and 1990s has shed light on its positivist heritage and re-shaped GT according to a constructivist perspective.
- Having identified the methodological disagreement between the two founders and briefly presented its features, over the last few years GT can be seen to have developed in three main directions or 'schools': (*a*) *classic or Glaserian* (Glaser); (*b*) *Straussian approach* (Strauss-Corbin); (*c*) *constructivist* (Charmaz), the differences of which are outlined earlier.

- Some critiques levelled at GT over the years are briefly presented here to show that there is an important critical debate going on in the academic community which scholars engaged in using this method should know about.

Further Readings

Historical Roots

Bryant, A., & Charmaz, K. (2007). *The SAGE Handbook of Grounded Theory*. Los Angeles, CA: SAGE, Chap. 1, pp. 31–57.

Morse, J. M. (2009). *Developing Grounded Theory: The Second Generation*. Walnut Creek: Left Coast (now Routledge, 2016). Contributions by Morse, J. M., Stern, P. N., Corbin, J. M., Bowers, B., Charmaz, K., & Clarke, A. E.

Pragmatism and Symbolic Interactionism

Aldiabat, K. M., & Le Navenec, C. L. (2011). Philosophical Roots of Classical Grounded Theory: Its Foundations in Symbolic Interactionism. *The Qualitative Report*, 16 (4), 1063–80.. Retrieved from http://www.nova.edu/ssss/QR/QR16-4/aldiabat.pdf

Bryant, A. (2009). Grounded Theory and Pragmatism: The Curious Case of Anselm Strauss. *Forum Qualitative Sozialforschung / Forum: Qualitative Social Research*, 10 (3), 1–31.

Bryant, A. (2017). *Grounded Theory and Grounded Theorizing: Pragmatism in Research Practice*. New York: Oxford University Press, part II.

Charmaz, K. (2008). The Legacy of Anselm Strauss in Constructivist Grounded Theory. In Norman K. Denzin, James Salvo, & Myra Washington (Eds.), *Studies in Symbolic Interaction (Studies in Symbolic Interaction, Volume 32)*, Emerald Group Publishing Limited, 127–41.

Kelle, U. (2007). The Development of Categories: Different Approaches in Grounded Theory. In A. Bryant, & K. Charmaz (Eds.), *The SAGE Handbook of Grounded Theory*. Los Angeles: Sage, 191–213, Chap. 9, p. 191.

GT in Various Research Areas

Artinian, B. M., Giske, T., & Cone, P. H. (2009). *Glaserian Grounded Theory in Nursing Research: Trusting Emergence*. New York: Springer Pub. Co.

Goulding, C. (2002). *Grounded Theory: A Practical Guide for Management, Business and Market Researchers*. London: Sage.

Henwood, K., & Pidgeon, N. (1996). Grounded Theory in Psychological Research. In P. M. Camic, J. E. Rhodes, & L. Yardley (Eds.), *Qualitative Research in Psychology: Expanding Perspectives in Methodology and Design*. Washington, DC: American Psychological Association, 131–55.

Hutchinson, S. A. (1988). Education and Grounded Theory. In Robert Sherman, & Rodman B. Webb (Eds.), *Qualitative Research in Education: Focus and Methods*. New York, NY: The Falmer Press.

Locke, K. (2001). *Grounded Theory in Management Research*. London: Sage.

Schreiber, R. S., & Stern, P. N. (2001). *Using Grounded Theory in Nursing*. New York: Springer Pub.

Wiener, C. L. (2004). *Grounded Theory in Medical Research from Theory to Practice* (Publications of the Helen Dowling Inst for Biopsychosocial Medicine, Vol. 2). London-New York: Routledge.

Further GT Developments

Bryant, A., & Charmaz, K. (2019). *The SAGE Handbook of Current Developments in Grounded Theory*. Los Angeles: SAGE.

3 The GT Process

3.1 The GT Journey

Travelling involves more than moving from one place to another. It entails more than simply sightseeing, moving and going. It is thanks to this 'something further' that the metaphor of travelling is effective in conveying GT processes with their sense of exploration, wonderment, curiosity, effort, adventure, uncertainty, disorientation and risk. Perhaps the GT journey no longer embodies the idea of discovery it once did: to conduct GT today is more reminiscent of a Chatwinian travel writer's journey than an Amundsen-style expedition. With the interpretative and postmodern turn in the social sciences, the journey of GT is perhaps less adventurous and extreme; at the same time, however, it is more responsive, reflective and observant of the entire landscape, fellow travellers and memory.

In fact, describing the GT journey in terms of its procedural aspect might just be the best way to help readers grasp the core of this methodology. The best way to understand *what* is often through *how*, and this is particularly true of GT as a methodology aimed at exploring processes that is in itself a process. It is not by chance or for practical reasons that this book chooses to emphasize the *doing* of GT, but because knowing how to do GT is the best route to comprehending its essence.

This chapter presents the stages and steps comprising a GT research process by arranging them in a summarizing diagram. The aim of the diagram is to convey the big picture, that is, the entire process, while the individual phases will be detailed more analytically in the rest of the volume.

Take heed, however. The abstract process with its logic and ideal progression cannot really be represented in a linear flow chart. What is more, it need not by any means be adopted once and for all or in one single way. The path research takes in the field is always uncertain, undulating; it cannot be planned meticulously beforehand. This is why doing research always involves some element of craftsmanship. It always calls for a certain un-plannable knowledge that helps researchers face the unexpected, something that cannot be corralled into rigid procedural sequences.

This fact does not exempt us from knowing each phase of the investigation process and being trained in its associated details, of course. It is best to keep in mind, however, that in actual practice the phases might look different and the apparent linearity in this presentation of the process, obviously adopted to improve explanatory clarity, is actually a regulative abstraction. In short, it is worthwhile to get trained in the ideal process of doing GT despite knowing that you will never encounter this ideal. Such training resembles the birthing classes offered at hospitals and free clinics. It is useful for future mothers (and fathers), especially those expecting their first child, to take part in one of these courses to anticipate how the delivery and steps leading up to it might go. It helps expectant parents to envisage and, thus, recognize and successfully manage the signs preceding and accompanying labour, the way delivery proceeds and the initial caretaking of the newborn, offering specific techniques to ensure the best experience with these steps. These courses can be highly reassuring precisely because they outline what is likely to happen and show that anyone, with adequate knowledge, can manage the inevitable crises with calm.

Describing the 'perfect process' through which delivery and labour unfold in all in its analytical detail might also be counterproductive, however. If it is presented (or taken) in an absolute and universal way, it ends up doing a disserve to new mothers, leading them to expect that same univocal linearity. In reality, of course, the fact is that every woman is different and so it is for every context; therefore, the perfect process they learnt about during the course never manifests as such. By outlining the process in an effort to reassure and help manage situations, such courses might run the risk of creating false expectations, disappointment and frustration, or even fear, when something does not take place exactly as it was presented in the classroom.

3.2 An Overview

To use a Socratic simile, the midwife's wisdom is more helpful in grasping the unfolding of the GT process than any detailed and analytical presentation of the ideal process. Nevertheless, let us look at Figure 3. Considering the chart in its entirety, three general elements immediately stand out:

1. The process is best represented by a spiral shape and specifically a helical spiral as opposed to a straight-linear one.
2. Some steps appear multiple times at increasing levels of abstraction along the expanding curves of the spiral.
3. It is not a regular and uniform trajectory: there are frequent steps backward and moments of regression as well as rapid accelerations and leaps ahead, with long periods of monotonous work alternating with phases of intense production and creation.

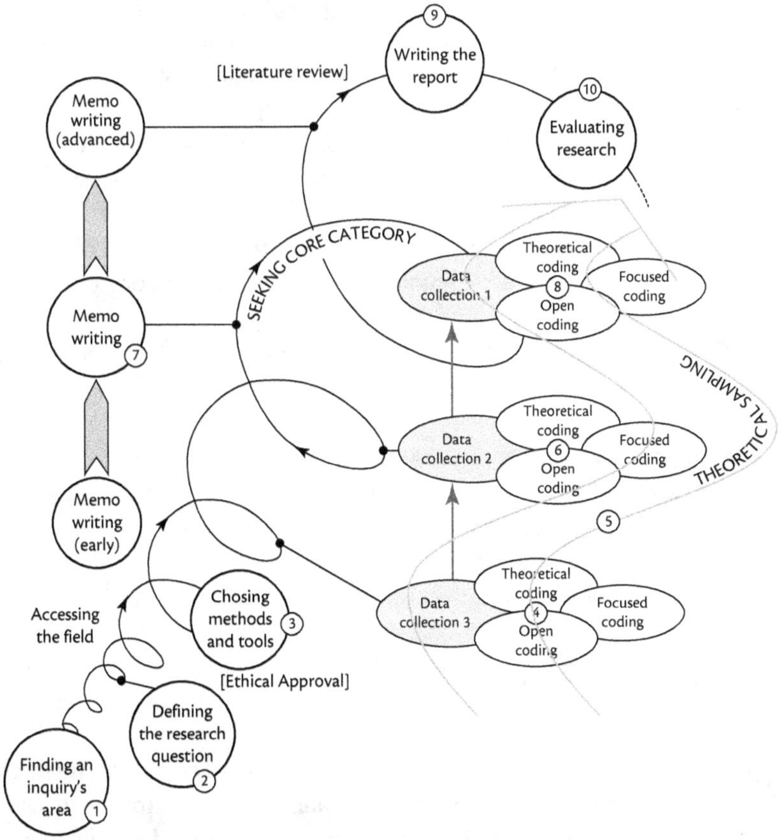

Figure 3 The GT process: Temporal and logical sequence.

The spiral shape indicates a virtuous circle. In this case, there is a development process that begins from a certain starting point and proceeds analytically, but not in a constant and ordered manner. Instead, it proceeds by returning again and again to certain steps, but each time at a different, higher level.

Given these premises, this chapter briefly presents the individual phases of the research process as synthesized in Figure 3 – that is, the stages of the journey of theory discovery/construction, in terms of their essential and procedural traits as part of the process. It then illustrates these steps by identifying them along the spiral of an actual research project conducted using the GT method, coordinated by the author (Tarozzi, 2007a). Excerpts from this research are presented in the text here using a different font. This approach of starting from a specific case to outline the individual steps serves to shed particular light on the elements of the process, elements which are not usually made explicit in a standard research report. The research, titled *TV family governance,* aimed to study TV consumption dynamics and practices in domestic contexts with children aged between three and six years old. Italy's Children and Television Board of Radio-TV Federation (FRT, a federation of about 150 local and private networks) commissioned the Department of Cognitive Sciences and Education (University of Trento) to conduct this study, and it was carried out by a multidisciplinary team of researchers from the Universities of Trento, Bologna and Naples. The team examined these dynamics and practices using an ethnographic approach. Although ethnography is thoroughly distinct from GT, it can nevertheless be complementary, especially when working in a constructivist perspective (Charmaz & Mitchell, 2001).

> The study was based on grounded theory and aimed at exploring processes of family television governance in homes with preschool children. Our topic was to explore three Italian cities (Trento, Bologna, and Naples) and to understand the processes at the root of basic television routine within family routine. In 2005, 15 families were visited 3 to 6 times each, and 5 other families were interviewed with a final semi-structured interview to evaluate the whole theory developed from the analysis.

In particular, this research was ethnographic in its data collection, research strategy, reference contexts, use of participant observation tools and close relationship with the research participants. GT instead determined the overall research design and, above all, the project's analytical procedures, data processing activities, theoretical sampling of subjects and the form of the final results.

Especially by virtue of its ethnographic approach to TV consumption, the profile of this research built on *cultural studies* of TV consumption (Morley, 1986; Lull, 1990). It was distinguished from this line of inquiry by the use of GT methodology, however, which steered the investigation towards the processes underlying the social, psychological and educational phenomena the researchers observed.

We gathered data in three different cities, observing a total of fifteen families (seven in Trento, four in Bologna and four in Napoli). We visited them three to six times each between February and June 2005, and five other families were given final, semi-structured interviews to evaluate the entire theory developed from the analysis. Each observation (sixty in total) required compiling extremely detailed field notes, highly descriptive and nonjudgmental, immediately after the visit.

The observation was participant, unstructured and took place in a home environment; generally, each period of observation lasted from 60 to 120 minutes. During the visit, the researcher interacted with the children, watched TV with them, played with them, spoke with their parents or other adult caretakers, and observed the settings. The team then conducted twenty-nine in-depth interviews, supplemented by five semi-structured interviews with parents and adult caretakers.

This chapter retraces the various stages of this study, presenting accounts based on the memos compiled during the course of the research. The accounts are descriptions from the inside, complete with all the hesitations, doubts and uncertainties usually left out of final research reports. Such a view from the inside helps to illustrate the procedural essence of the method. It is also important to begin with an overview so as to anticipate what might reasonably occur; a global view of this kind can help reduce researcher's anxiety and curb potential chaos. The key turning points of the research process will be outlined in more detail in the following chapters.

3.3 The 9 Stages of the GT Journey

3.3.1 Identifying an Area of Research

GT does not begin from hypotheses, derived from a meticulous analysis of the literature or previous empirical studies, that the researcher intends to test. Unlike other qualitative research studies, it likewise does not commence from specific and focused objectives. It instead develops out of the desire or need to explore a research area, taken in all of its entirety and complexity, without immediately reducing it to a few controllable variables or an excessively precise research question.

Symbolic interactionism (Blumer, 1954, 1969) suggests that inquiry begins from *sensitizing concepts*, that is, sociological concepts that do not confine reality within closed, predetermined or operationalizable views. Sensitizing concepts are understood instead as 'open' concepts that guide the researcher without forcing the data to fit inside fixed sociological boxes (Bowen, 2006) (see Chapter 4, section 4.2.1). Such concepts represent the background ideas against which research problems stand out. In terms of the way knowledge about a certain area is organized, sensitizing concepts are research starting points rather than end points that corral social reality within closed boxes. Indeed, research questions expressed in non-sensitizing concepts show that there is already a pre-existing theory providing a language and narrowing the research focus.

> In the case of the research presented as an example, ideas such as 'TV experience', especially, and 'children's TV competence' constituted sensitising concepts from which the research could develop. Such ideas and the general area of interest, namely the theme of relationships between TV and children, corresponded to the personal and professional interests of the author as they had been the target of various previous studies and reflected the author's focus, during training, on critical and conscious consumption as well as consultancy work in the production of children's programmes and the regulation of TV.

3.3.2 *Defining the Generative Research Question*

See Section 4.2

Translating a *research area* (or *theme*) into a *research question* (or *problem*) is one of the most complex and delicate stages of the entire qualitative research process. Although the various orientations understand the research question in substantially different ways (cfr. Chapters 2 and 4), the research question at the beginning of a GT trajectory is a generative, an open and not excessively focused question. It essentially boils down to Glaser's well-expressed phrase, 'What's going on here?' Or, in other words, what happens in a certain area of interest in more or less binding relation to some phenomena or concepts judged to be relevant.

The significance of this choice is particularly clear for GT. Here, a precise formulation of the research problem cannot be established in advance because doing so would force the data based on prior knowledge; instead, the research question should serve as a tool for allowing researchers to 'listen' to the data with open minds and allowing the data to guide them towards a theory that can then be formulated retrospectively.

> In the initial project, the research question was not formulated very precisely; after preliminary immersion in the field, it was defined as: 'What happens in domestic contexts where there are children aged 3-6 in relation to the TV experience?'. The formulation of this question was kept deliberately open, using the term domestic contexts and not family (which would refer to just one institution), specifying a concept considered relevant (children aged 3-6, because these represented a new audience bracket only recently discovered by broadcasters), and using the sensitising concept of 'TV experience'.
>
> It was not only loyalty to the method that drove us to enter the field with an open and broad research question. The requests of the client, interpreted as ambiguous and contradictory, also suggested this direction. The committee that had commissioned the research, consisting of representatives of TV broadcasters and child, consumer or family protection associations, encompassed divergent expectations and expectations about the outcomes of the research: each of them, as often happens, expected an empirical scientific confirmation of their own beliefs which, in relation to the relationship between children and TV, are rather fixed and highly ideologically oriented.

Adopting an ideological perspective involving pre-defined notions instead of sensitizing concepts would have led the team to formulating a research question that already corresponded to a specific, determined perspective. This is precisely the critique Glaser made about Strauss and Corbin's approach, arguing that starting from highly defined and focused research questions generates descriptive results, aimed at verifying hypothesis rather than theory building. Such an approach thus confirms the researchers' preconceived ideas, ideas which are more or less implicit in the initial question and categories.

3.3.3 Ethical Approval

See Section 4.3

When using GT, it is not always easy to obtain approval from the ethics committee of a research institution. The problem lies in the fact that only the very first phases can be planned with precision; afterwards, GT practitioners cannot know the exact number of participants who will be included in the sample, define the structure of the interviews, predict how the questions will evolve or even know if it will prove necessary to collect further data through strategies not foreseen at the beginning. The theoretical sampling addressed in section 5.2. guides both the approach to and scope of data collection as well as sample size, based on the concepts that gradually emerge from the analysis. Filling out forms for ethical approval, however, requires applicants to accurately predict the research procedures they will adopt so that the committee or supervisors can approve them. By now many supervisors are aware of the particular nature of GT and other inductive and theory-building research methods. Therefore, they will be willing to accept that a relative lack of information stems from the nature of the method and not from any ethical inattention or negligence on the part of the researcher. There is a practical solution, however, and it consists in presenting an estimated surplus scenario and specifying extremely accurate interview protocols. It is more ethically conscientious and thus definitely preferable to obtain approval for a larger number of interviews and more precise and invasive interview protocols than will actually be carried out.

3.3.4 Deciding on Data Collection Methods and Tools

See Section 4.4

Many types of data can be useful for GT research, and there are various tools and methods for collecting them. The methods should not be seen as neutral in relation to the data; however, each tool has a specific impact on the type of data the study will gather and it is important to be aware of these implications. Observations, ethnographic field notes, participants' personal accounts, narratives and even documents can all offer data which are rich and useful, but always moulded by the tool used to collect them. The main but not the only tool used in GT is interviewing, especially the semi-structured interviews. GT practitioners continue to prefer interviews because of their emphasis on the attribution of meanings typical of symbolic interactionism, but also because verbal instruments are flexible enough to allow researchers to focus data collection according to their coding. As the theory emerges and the researcher proceeds with theoretical sampling and formulating the emerging categories, the interviews thus become increasingly structured: the interviews begin as very unstructured (but never completely open) and gradually end up with more specifically defined questions.

Working in a team and comparing the different ways in which the same tools can be applied can help foster core awareness about the effect of enacting the methods. Conducting the research in a team, instead of individually, is preferable in many ways as the comparison amongst different perspectives, views, disciplinary interests, and competences, if managed well, can represent a further area of constant dialogue and sharing and thereby further enrich the coding and analysis work. In this case, it was necessary to envisage a phase for the group to train in and share about the tools they employed. This was the case with our research, in which the team was constituted by people with different training, from different areas of Italy, and with different professional competences. After an initial negotiating phase (June-December) with the funding body, methodologically important for defining the breadth, priority, and approach of the research, we set up a research team that allowed us to carry out the research simultaneously in three different Italian cities. The following January there was a residential seminar to share the research project and train the researchers on the chosen research methodology. This occasion also served to harmonise and calibrate diverse theoretical orientations and adopt common tools (after having also tested them through negotiation processes) for data collection.

In our example, since we used observational tools and field work, it was also necessary to practise observational skills which, given the nature of the method, could not be based on establishing rigid and excessively structured observational protocols. Trial interviews and discussions about how to carry out and transcribe them, so as to agree on the transcription criteria, were conducted for in-depth interviews as well. It is difficult in this case to define rigid protocols ahead of time

> or to establish suitable tools for investigating the generative research question once and for all. Rather than rigidly detailing the protocols (which do, however, need to be determined), it is thus necessary for everyone to exercise his or her theoretical sensibility and to negotiate this among the team members.

At the same time, the researcher proceeds by selecting the first subjects and accessing the field. Theoretical sampling requires starting with an initial group of subjects identified through purposive sampling and progressively extending this group based on stimuli from the emerging theory. Therefore, the process of locating participants and securing their consent to participate in the research becomes increasingly complex and sensitive as the choice of subjects comes to be delimited by the directions suggested by the analysis. When the research in question is an ethnography, as in the example presented here, accessing the field is even more sensitive. Although an ethnographic approach can be particularly intrusive in itself, the relationship the researcher builds with participants is nevertheless crucial for generating rich data.

> Approaching participants took place through gate keepers, third parties (at the beginning, friends' friends or, in some cases, the nursery school), who introduced the researcher to the family in whose house we intended to conduct observation. Everything was carried out in full respect of the ethical code of the department coordinating the research and the participants, who signed a detailed informed consent form, were given the chance to contact the ethics committee directly.

3.3.5 *Data Collection and Coding*

See Chapter 5

Having established and formed the group, communicated the research tools and approaches, identified the first group of subjects and obtained the necessary ethical approval, the researcher can access the field with all the required sensitivity by clearly bearing in mind the generative research question. By this point, several months have already passed (eight months, in our case). The research should not be envisaged as beginning only when the audio-recorder is turned on and the first face-to-face interview is initiated. The work carried out in the prior phases, from negotiating the research question with funders to developing the research design, from identifying and forming the research team to selecting the first subjects and units of analysis and accessing the field, constitutes the theory-generating activity. All of this material is ripe for recording meaningful reflections in the research diary and developing the first, early examples of memos – the typical analytical and reflective thinking tools I will discuss further in section 3.3.8.

Data collection/coding takes place through a number of steps. The first collection/coding step characterized by broad, diversified data and mainly open coding is followed by a second step. Here, the researcher ideally collects fewer but more focused data and privileges advanced coding phases. By following the directions of theoretical sampling, subsequent data collection becomes more focused, with the interview questions more structured and targeted and the observer's gaze more sensitized and centred on pertinent themes. The third step requires very precise data based on the conceptualizations that have emerged thus far, rather quick moments of open coding using codes which by now are well established (but still open to allow unexpected elements to emerge) and lingering on phases of more advanced, focused and theoretical coding using categories which by that point have been more fully identified and the connections among them largely mapped. In some cases, three steps will provide enough analytical processing to outline the theory; in others, further collection/analysis stages may be necessary. In any case, it is really impossible to envisage the future development of the design in its entirety from the beginning of the research process. Rather, GT practitioners should be prepared to undertake an explorative journey in which, after the first predictable steps, the continued unfolding of the research process is determined by whatever they find at the end of each stage.

One distinctive trait of GT is that data collection, interviewing and observation take place simultaneously with coding. Do not wait until most of all of the interviews have been conducted before facing the laborious job of transcription and analysis. In GT, it is crucial for these processes to take place alongside each other. Initial coding helps to identify the themes that will be addressed in the following interviews, and it is fundamental that researchers identify the directions in which the sample should be expanded, write up their first reflections in memos and make space for insight to emerge, as may occur at any time, even the first phases of the research.

Coding, the first level of the analytical process, can be summarized as the set of techniques and procedures used to conceptualize data. These techniques and procedures assume different names and suggest different processes in the various GT traditions, but always within a common logic. The first coding operation, the zero level of analysis, is interview transcription itself. Transcription should not be regarded as a boring yet essentially simple and automatic job that could just as easily be delegated to the increasingly reliable transcription software now available. Instead, transcription is always an interpretative task even when using rigid transcription guidelines, and it represents an integral part of coding.

Initial coding (section 5.1.1): The transcription is followed by open coding with its analytical procedures that call on the researcher to proceed word by word, line by line and incident by incident (Glaser, 1978). These procedures *open up* the text so that all the possible interpretative directions might emerge (this step is also called 'open coding') by identifying minimal meaning units – namely, the shortest segments of text that are considered meaningful – and then assigning them a nominal label. This endeavour is often highly frustrating and plagued by angst, consisting as it does of conceptualizing the relevant textual excerpts without forcing the text to conform to preconceptions and by remaining at a very descriptive level. Nothing seems to emerge and the few ideas the researcher had at the beginning may even become foggy and uncertain. Indeed, the research problem itself is called into question by the chaotic stimuli flowing from the field.

> On the basis of the first bulk of data considered valid, about two weeks after the first launch meeting we proceeded with an open/initial coding, working in pairs on the same material. The process included two stages: the first consisted in identifying those parts of text considered meaningful, the minimal meaning units that encompassed a concept; the second one, distinct from the first, involved assigning a name to the identified codes. Assigning a name to an interpretive code requires staying faithful to the intentionality of the speaker and not imposing denominations that operate to characterise in too rigid a way, such as terms inferred from the literature on the theme. For this reason, especially in the first phase we favoured so-called 'in vivo' coding, which uses the speaker's own words to name the codes whenever possible. Since faithfulness to the text (to the phenomenon) was a priority, the names for the

categories developed in the open/initial coding were necessarily very broad, long, and difficult to connect to each other, very difficult to manage and rather messy overall. Then an intense and thorough discussion meeting followed, aimed not so much at reaching what could be defined an inter-coder agreement (in part because there are no possible indexes to measure that) as to enable the emergence of the first categories which, in following visits, would guide the researcher's gaze specifically towards those specific themes that had started to surface from different contexts.

3.3.6 *Theoretical Sampling*

See Section 5.2

In qualitative research, the meaning of sampling, that is, the criteria used to select participants, is quite unlike the probabilistic sampling that constitutes a key stage for ensuring the validity of a quantitative study. Nevertheless, qualitative researchers cannot circumvent the sampling problem. It is a matter that must be addressed, albeit certainly differently depending on whether the research is more or less descriptive; researchers will need to formulate an answer to this issue that is coherent with the research approach they have chosen and comprehensible for the research community to whom the study is directed.

GT proposes a type of rigorous but not probabilistic sampling for qualitative research. It is not aimed at ensuring the representativeness of the group of subjects as determined in relation to the total population; rather, it is above all a precious tool that guides and clarifies the analytical process. Theoretical sampling consists in identifying research subjects by pursuing the directions that surface during the process of analysis. In particular, it is necessary to continuously delve deeper in response to ongoing gaps in the theory. The purpose of such focused follow-up is to ascertain whether the draft theory and its categories continue to hold up, including in contexts differing from those examined, wherever the researcher finds those specific conditions in which the theory appears to be lacking.

As section 5.2 will show, theoretical sampling in GT is more than a smart procedure for selecting participants. Indeed, theoretical sampling can be regarded as a device for representing the phenomenon, not the population (Morse & Clark, 2019).

The expansion of the sample is complete when the categories or concepts that emerged in relation to a given theme are considered *saturated* (Morse, 1995). In other words, theoretical sampling requires the researcher to extend the sample scope towards those areas that can be seen to be uncovered, whereas there is no need to do additional sampling for areas in which the data are already redundant. This approach saves time and resources as compared to statistical sampling, but it prevents users from defining *a priori* the number of participants, settings, interviews or observations, with all of the above-mentioned repercussions on one's ability to formulate a detailed research design in advance.

> The research started from an already-differentiated sample because we assumed that there were different conditions in different socio-cultural and geographic contexts. Trento, Bologna and Napoli constituted three contexts differentiated according to geographical location (North, Centre and South of Italy) and the dimensions of the urban context (small town, medium and big city). We made this choice a priori for merely organisational reasons: with the funding constraints, we needed to arrange the team in advance so as to take distant geographical contexts into consideration. Proper, by-the-book theoretical sampling would have instead required we start from a setting and widen the sample only if and when the ideas emerging from the analysis required it. Widening the sample a priori is not in itself a methodological mistake, but in fact it forces us to collect data that might prove unnecessary, and we thus waste time, energy and resources. And indeed, in hindsight, we did not find the kind of significant differences among small and medium that would have justified this sample differentiation; in contrast, the North-South difference represented an important 'variable' in the sample, in managing family routines.
>
> We then extended the sample over time to include one-parent families, settings in which fathers were also actively present, homes with satellite and/or cable TV, homes in which target children were both male and female, etc. Above all, however, the adoption of this type of sampling actually fostered a key stage for theoretical development: after a first bulk of interviews and observations from which emerged a first draft theory on family TV governance according to which mothers played a key role in this task, having observed primarily people who had good cultural and educational tools for TV governance, we asked ourselves whether this depended

> on cultural and socio-economic levels. We thus noticed that this kind of information in particular was missing from the number of families observed up to that point. Therefore, we further widened the sample in the direction of families with low socio-economic positions and with a low level of TV control and rule development.

Data collection and focused coding (section 5.1.4). The coding carried out in this phase is located on a higher analytical level: the mainly descriptive and substantive level of initial coding is left behind and some, albeit promising, tracks which in the previous coding were left open to conform to suggestions from the data are closed. The salient themes are allowed to surface in this phase along with, here but especially in the following steps, the categories inductively drawn from the data and labelling operations.

In this phase, the GT user examines the larger excerpts of text that arise more frequently or with more intensity, encompass more relevant analytical meanings and suggest directions for categorizing the data in a more incisive and complete way (Charmaz, 2014). Above all, however, in this phase the codes that emerged from initial coding are combined with each other in the pursuit of proto-categories characterized by a higher degree of abstraction. This operation opens up a space for the main directions, themes and interpretative categories (although still expressed in an approximate manner) indicated by the data to emerge.

> This phase of the analysis is characterized by two moments. An individual moment in which each researcher has developed his or her own interviews and observations on the basis of the initial coding and, subsequently, another moment in which focused coding is compared as a group to identify the themes that emerged more frequently or more forcefully. At the end of this long phase of data collection and analysis (about ten families), a marathon meeting allowed the group to thoroughly discuss all the categories which had emerged individually up to that point to develop a first shared coding map in which all the themes that had emerged from each context were represented and no theme was excluded, although perhaps expressed in different terms than those with which the encoder had initially named it. What surfaced was an intricate and complex picture that provided the first chaotic yet complete description in the complex of themes that had emerged from the families observed. The

themes were all present, but not well developed, and the relationships among them were likewise only purely hypothesized. Nevertheless, this coding allowed the team to start formulating a draft theory by abandoning themes that, although present, were marginal in relation to the more mainstream ones, to better focus the research question, and to identify the matters worth exploring further in the following round of data collection and the most effective ways to do it (for instance, how to bypass parents' tendency to self-represent themselves as 'good parents' by answering our questions in ways they thought matched our expectations).

3.3.7 *Writing Memos*

See Section 6.1

Memos are a distinctive trait of every GT. Given that they appear in various phases of the research process, it is difficult to assign them a single, precise place within the spiral that illustrates the GT journey. At the focused coding stage, for instance, some memos have already been written. The researcher will need to clarify his or her observations on conducting interviews, reflections guiding theoretical sampling choices, and the notes that inevitably accompany the act of formulating the labels in initial or focused coding in a discursive manner. These observations and reflections must be justified analytically without taking anything for granted. Memos accompany the entire process of theory building and it is fundamental that they serve as a place in which nothing is taken for granted, in which users justify every single choice or action and begin to give shape to their arguments. Memos are not metareflective research diaries (these two tools may coincide but only partially and at certain moments), nor are they an intimate space for researchers to jot down personal comments. They are likewise not ethnographic fieldnotes. Their specificity is that they constitute *spaces of analysis* in which researchers account for the research's key hubs, critical stages, theoretical sampling choices, the questions that are asked of the data and the categories through which and the reasons according to which these questions are given suitable answers.

Memos appear multiple times along the spiral of GT, and they assume a specific role depending on the function that they carry out at each different stage. Charmaz distinguishes between early and advanced memos by characterizing the former as a critical and reflective complement to data collection that serve to explore and clarify the researcher's choices about the first phases of coding and to guide subsequent interviews and observations; the latter, more analytically powerful memos, account for the categorization process, for how the categories emerged. Such memos trace the analytical path of these categories, describing their properties and helping the GT practitioner reflect on what the initial outcomes mean for the participants and so on (Charmaz, 2014). It is thus clear that memos play an intermediate role between data collection and report writing. Indeed, the report writing is based precisely on a systematic examination of the more advanced memos which, if they have been written systematically and regularly, potentially already contain a large portion of the final write-up.

> We used memos related to the emerging thoughts after the observations and interviews. We have memos that accompanied the initial coding work and memos that systematize the thinking that emerged in the moments of sudden interpretative acceleration. These memos are written by individual members of the team and then shared with the rest of the team, especially some longer and more systematic ones that we decided to write in particular moments of breakthrough. They accompany the emergence of the theory and facilitate the process of identifying links and engaging in theoretical abstraction.
>
> We fostered the production of memos after each team meeting, in which the sharing of an individual viewpoint on the analysis converged, more or less harmoniously, into a viewpoint that was collective and shared across all of the theory-building. These, together with the reports of group discussions (these were also systematically recorded), were precious materials that documented the stages that took place and drove the conceptual building process forward by indicating new lines of investigation for data collection and by forming the basis of the first conceptual systematization of the coding map.

Theoretical coding (section 5.1.5). I use the term 'theoretical coding' to mean the analytical process of data conceptualization that occurs at a more abstract level. In particular, this is the level of analysis in which the researcher specifies and further identifies the relationships among the categories that have emerged from focused coding. It is the level on which the theory takes shape, the categories are integrated and the analytical fog that accompanied the first phases of coding, necessarily open to the endless input flowing from the field, starts to dissipate in favour of a coherent interpretative theory. It is the moment in which the theory takes off. Theory, at this stage, clearly detaches itself from the descriptive level and proceeds through increasing acts of conceptual abstraction. This is an extremely complex and non-linear phase formed of intuitions, leaps forward and moments of returning to the data.

Some insights do already emerge from the first steps of collection/analysis; however, due to their nature the theoretical coding strategies are more effective and appropriate in the more advanced stages, based on advanced, focused codes.

This analytical stage has been named and described in various ways by the different schools, each with somewhat different procedures, but it involves four fundamental steps:

1. developing the categories;
2. connecting the categories with each other;
3. identifying the core category;
4. integrating and defining the theory.

I outline each passage in more depth next (more details can be found in section 5.1.5)

1. *Developing the categories.* The focused coding has produced some proto-categories, but these are still quite rough. The scope of the theoretical coding is to define these proto-categories more accurately. The search for the *core categor(ies)*, the central category I will address in more depth later, is what guides this process. It is this search that grants direction to the analysis and prevents the theoretical coding from scattering in a thousand different directions, each in pursuit of their own individual sense.

At this stage the categories take shape and, especially, receive a proper name. The names of such categories should be dynamic and open, with elevated connotative and evocative power. In English, a language which is much more conceptualizing than other neo-Latin languages, researchers are advised to use a noun combined with a gerund. The noun defines the object while the verb suggests its conceptual movement. Some examples of categories of this type include 'TV as order producer', 'controlling the TV', 'TV as drug'. It is also important to make the effort to define each category in a way that goes beyond title alone by providing an extended description that renders it explicitly comprehensible.

> The theoretical analysis of the complex conceptual map that surfaced from the focused coding has highlighted some thematic cores, each widely branching, that could be extrapolated from the overall picture. Each takes on its own semantic and conceptual meaning even while maintaining some or many links with other thematic cores. These themes, subsequently re-elaborated and confirmed by the new data collected, produced four important, fundamental, recurrent, dense, branching categories that stand out over the other categories which also emerged and were defined:
>
> - *media-environment*: the mediatic system and available technologies viewed in terms of their use and the impact that they have on family routines;
> - *TV governance*: the intervention strategies that regulate ways of using and controlling TV consumption and the value system and naive pedagogies on which it is based. A category that can be see right away to constitute a macro category, wider and more branching than the others;
> - *judgments about TV*: the set of judgments about the various aspects of TV fruition and viewing options seen in terms of their implications for the system of rules that derive from them;
> - *fruition of TV*: the TV routines generated by the various ways of using TV that intertwine with family routines by generating or adjusting to them.

2. *Linking the categories (relationships and hierarchy).* The categories produced by the comparative analysis emerge together with the relationships that link them. Indeed, such categories are only comprehensible to the researcher as part of the networks of relationships in which they are embedded. In theoretical coding, the analysis of these relationships is a fundamental stage which in turn comprises three different operations:

- linking the categories with each other and thematizing the type of relationship that connects them;
- developing (deductively and not inductively) the categories, with subcategories based on the properties and the size of each one;

- placing the categories in a hierarchical relationship by identifying macro categories that subsume smaller categories.

> We then attempted to create an initial conceptual link among similar categories by identifying both sibling-concepts and child-concepts, understanding the former as an initial vertical hierarchical arrangement and the latter as horizontal relationships of varying nature. On the basis of these formulations we built an initial conceptual pyramid that led us to the identification of the core category, the category that stood out as the main relevant theme in the area under investigation.

3. *Identifying the core category.* Working with conceptual maps allows GT users to illustrate the system in which each category is located. Drawing diagrams is a valid tool of analysis that facilitates the work of identifying the *core category*, as can be inferred from Figure 4: the core category or *core variable* is that central category that represents the main organizing concept in a research area. This organizing concept can be identified inductively by arranging the categories that have emerged from the data hierarchically. However, a core category appears suddenly as the result of insight rather than emerging from progressive acts of induction.

A core category is a key category with its own branches. It is often the category that appeared most frequently in the data, but it is especially the most analytically powerful one. It is dense, saturated and capable of bringing the theory together; it is also complete, relevant and functional in the sense of working. To find it, researchers may use devices such as diagrams and narratives of the research story. Such devices offer an integrated reading of the concepts expressed by the various categories which have as yet been highly fragmented.

> While we completed the data collection with families (it was the end of June), in light of the discussions we had and the materials we produced, it became clear that we needed to wrap up what had been produced up to that point. In this phase, a meeting with Barney Glaser was timely. Two of us met him in Stockholm, on the margins of a sociology convention in which the author had the opportunity to discuss the research framework and some preliminary outcomes with Glaser. Before the meeting we had restructured the initial confusing diagram, reorganised the categories in the space, removed

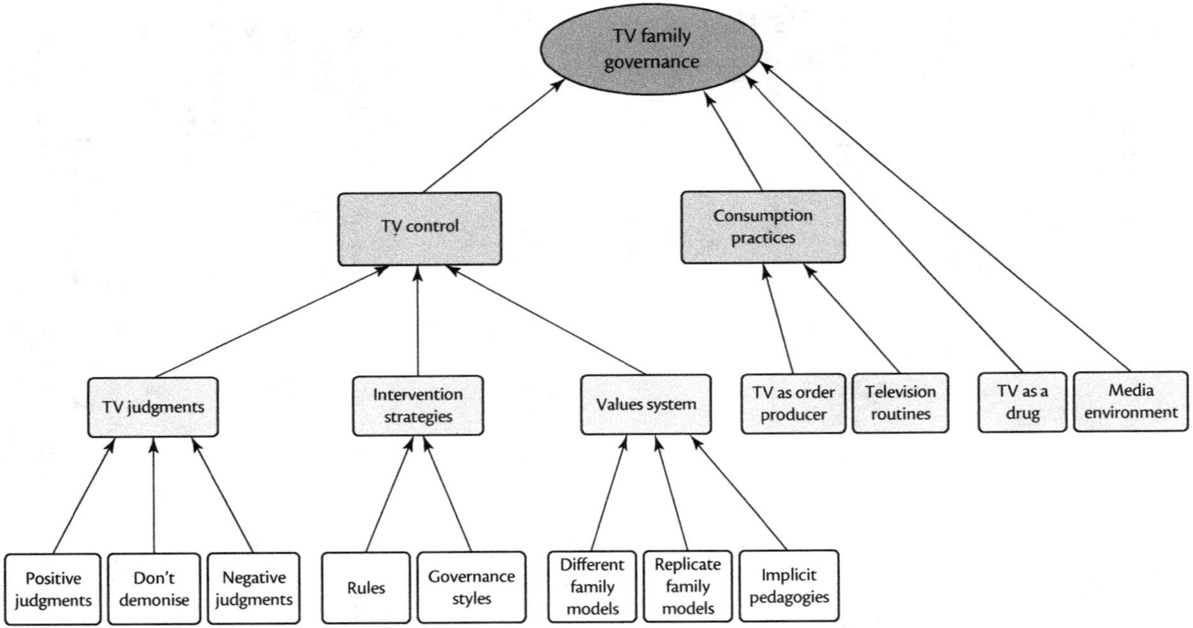

Figure 4 Hierarchical organization of the categories and identification of the core category.
Source: M. Tarozzi (2007a, p. 42).

some repetitions, translated them into English (and, therefore, necessarily re-interpreted them). This led us to identify some primary areas (although it also required removing many others from the spotlight of heuristic attention): we were not yet able to identify the core category precisely and, especially, did not yet know what to call it, but we could indicate the area in our conceptual map where it was located.

Preparing for the seminar, the suggestions received there, and the reflections developed in the period following those important discussions triggered a significant step forward with coding. After the Stockholm seminar, the author stopped and wrote the first working paper, a long memo which gathered together and systematized the analyses that had emerged from the memos written by everyone up to that point and indicated the first interpretative leads. We then proceeded by merging the memos, diagrams, coding and narratives. We also reflected on the coding system used, the branches among the concepts and categories, the memos produced by all the team members, and the labels that had emerged from the focused coding and briefly returned to the data, although more in search of confirmations than inspiration. As a result, we were able to name the core category as *TV family governance*. This broad concept that refers to the process of TV governance underlying TV consumer and fruition practices.

4. *Integrating and defining the theory.* The research work is not finished once the core category has been identified, however. A GT is a theoretical formulation conducted on the basis of the data for one or more processes that occur in a certain context. Therefore, the task remains of demarcating the theory's scope of validity and, hence, identifying (at this point, very accurately) the research question. The research question can only be fully defined at the point the research is ready to provide an answer to it.

Having identified the central category, *TV family governance*, the other, albeit interesting, lines of research lapse and completely evaporate. For example, the *media environment* and other themes, although promising, are only retained in terms of their link with the core category.

This step involves further analytical elaboration of the basic social process by carrying out new comparisons and interrogating the categories and data that generated them in a different way in order to then integrate the categories and properties into a single interpretative model.

> In the research, the identification of the core category gives rise to new research questions with which to consider the data, both those already collected and those from the new families being observed. The author asked in a memo: 'Are there different styles of TV family governance? Different ways of managing rules? Where do the rules come from? What are the attributes and characteristics of what to this point we have called "naive pedagogies"? What is their rootedness in an explicit value system? What relationship, if any (the first impression is that there is not always a direct correlation), exists between the judgments and the rules? On what basis is a judgement considered negative or positive? What influence does the personal history of the reference adults have in determining the character of the judgments and consequent intervention strategies?'
>
> New analytical tasks are required as well, on the basis of these new questions: defining properties and attributes to the emerging categories; verifying whether all of them can be considered saturated; redefining the theoretical sampling towards the not-yet-saturated categories; and developing the processes underlying the core category and identifying its attributes (sub-categories) and relationships with the other categories.
>
> By outlining the characteristics and attributes of each category and, especially, the conceptual and meaning links that connect them to each other and to the core category, it is possible to being sketching an interpretative theory explaining the phenomenon summarized by the core category.

After a total immersion in the analytical activity of coding the interviews and observations so that all the codes related to the identified themes can emerge and new thematic cores can surface, this process requires the supreme effort of linking the categories and themes that have emerged into a (single) model that corresponds to the core category and explains the theoretical process connecting all of them. This is a peculiar operation and distinct from the previous ones. Specifically, it moves back and forth from induction to deduction, analysis and synthesis. On the basis of the core category, this operation develops the main nodes, concepts and relations of the core category and unpacks the procedural elements which give rise to the general theory (see Figure 5).

> In moving from the inductive work of coding to the more theoretical work of integrating the categories and their properties with each other, thus detaching oneself from the data and working conceptually with the emergent macro categories, the author was struck by an insight. He thus drew a model on paper which synthetically represented the main process found in our area of investigation.

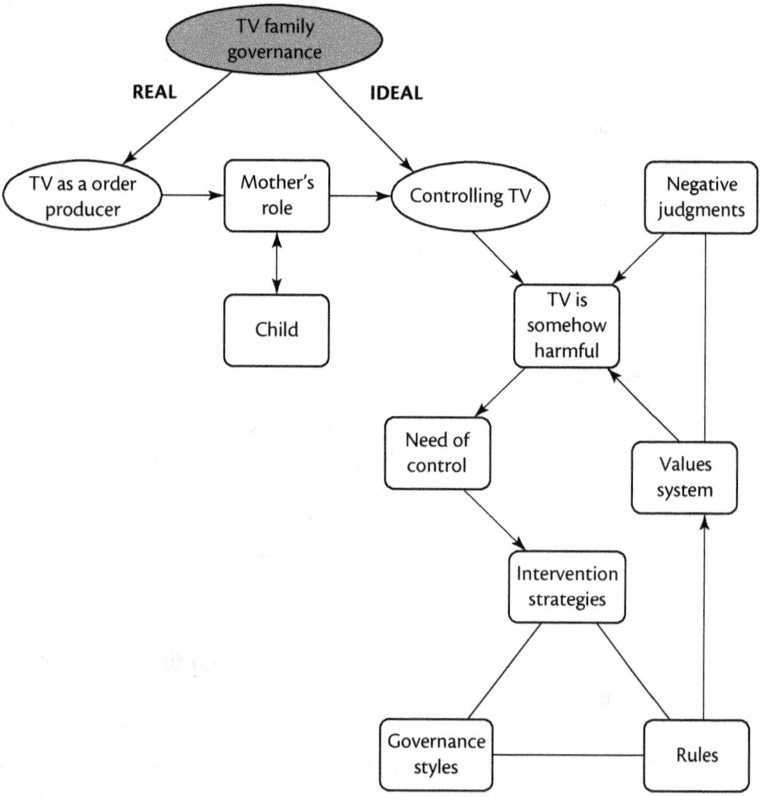

Figure 5 General diagram of the TV family governance.
Source: Tarozzi (2007, p. 47).

This model holds everything together; it is effective, empirically sound, simple and aesthetically beautiful. The process (or processes) that link the concepts are developed in this model, and it gives rise to an explanatory model that places the core category side by side with another key category, 'TV as order producer', which underpins another process (one we named 'real') that is juxtaposed to the 'ideal' process of TV control.

3.3.8 *Writing the Report*

See Chapter 6

A great advantage of doing GT consists in the fact that the writing process does not happen at the end, but rather accompanies all the phases of research. Writing the report involves starting from one's own advanced memos; the researcher seeks to arrange them systematically and is often able to include most of them in their entirety.

In turn, the writing process can be seen as a further, final, level of analysis. Since writing is always also interpreting, writing is a sophisticated conceptualizing and meaning-making process. Indeed, the theory takes through the act of (scientific) writing. The final write-up in GT requires the researcher to account for the process, not just the product. It is thus desirable that the written report include a lengthy and thorough section explaining the research process and outlining the temporal evolution of the process through which the theory emerged.

Although all GT manuals indicate writing strategies and techniques typical of this method (Charmaz, 2014; Corbin & Strauss, 2015; Urquhart, 2013; Gibson & Hartman, 2014), there are no writing procedures which are unique to GT, as with other phases of the GT journey. Nonetheless, some directions may prove useful (cfr. Chapter 6).

Especially according to a constructivist approach, it is in writing that the analytical power of theorizing takes shape and is articulated in all of its forms. It is in writing that the meanings, actions and social structures are discursively integrated. This is also the site in which the results which have emerged from the research are brought into empirical dialogue with the academic literature. In the first chapter, I mentioned the debate surrounding opportunities for engaging with the scientific literature and how to manage such engagement. Especially when writing for publication, whether a scientific article that has to be reviewed by an editorial committee or a doctoral thesis that must be assessed by an examining board, there is no avoiding engagement with the existing literature. A reasonable solution is to return to the library when the theory is sufficiently developed and allow the results to engage with the relevant scientific literature on the given theme just before preparing to write.

> The writing phase produced first a report and then an edited volume (Tarozzi, 2007a) which, after an introduction tracing the genesis of the theory in a diachronic way, addressed the process of TV family governance both in terms of TV control and in reference to the use of TV as a producer of order. The volume did so by clarifying the key stages and main conceptual turning points and presenting the general model complete with its overall developments. Various chapters followed in which each member of the team developed a specific theme of the general model to address the main themes which had emerged from the research in more detail. In particular, such themes included the question of judgments about TV, intervention strategies, styles of TV family governance and the role of the mother, the person who stands out in this complex context as the central and fundamental figure. Finally, the outcomes of the research were connected to some of the elements identified in the scientific literature on the theme in order to highlight their congruences and divergences and to shed light on the main operational and practical outcomes.
>
> The language and explanatory style of that report tried, in some ways, to reproduce the process of analysis that characterized our research, starting from the narrative style characterising the introduction. This was the only way to account for the procedural elements so inseparable from the research style, itself inspired by the paradigm and methodology that we outlined.

3.3.9 *Evaluating the Research*

See Section 6.4

Unlike many other qualitative research methods, GT does not require external validation. According to the principle of modifiability, one of the elements characterizing this methodology, as outlined by Glaser (1978), is that it self-corrects. If something appears to be incorrect, inaccurate or incomplete, its categories not adequately saturated or the associated theoretical sampling limited, and so on, such a fact does not discredit or falsify the theory. It simply represents a chance to extend or correct it. Nevertheless, as with all other qualitative research, the significance of GT outcomes can be reinforced through forms of external validation. One such is the audit trail (Lincoln & Guba, 1985), which allows a competent external researcher to retrace the descriptive and conceptual process undertaken by the original researcher (as long as the procedures are designed from the outset to be transparent) and thereby verify how appropriate the chosen tools were and how correctly the method's procedures were employed, as well as confirming whether or not they generate the same results.

> As a verification of the 'solidity' of the draft theory and to increase the transferability of the results, in October we conducted five more semi-structured interviews in which we asked the new subjects targeted questions based on the developed theory, to verify whether the same considerations were valid in those contexts as well.
>
> We offered our colleagues at the International Institute of Qualitative Methodology the opportunity to access the data gathered and the coding carried out and to retrace the analytical process conducted by the research team. This lengthy exchange, along with the external evaluation by Glaser, represented a sort of confirmation, a critical friendly evaluation. It was not a real audit of the reliability of the procedures and credibility of the results which had emerged until then. Nonetheless, even if not necessary, such verification can only help reinforce the validity of the proposed theory.

Towards a Formal Theory

The nine-stage trajectory outlined so far produced a complete, substantive theory; however, on a broader sociological view, this theory could also be extended. A further, optional step to extend the GT journey is that of producing a formal theory. Glaser and Strauss distinguish between *substantive theory*, which interprets and explains a specific problem in one particular substantive area, and *formal theory*, which instead offers a second-level interpretation of a theme or general process involving multiple substantive areas. If for instance a GT proposes a substantive theory on status shift in hospital settings in relation to dying, it is possible to then build a formal theory on status shift (Glaser & Strauss, 1971), at an even broader level of generalization, that theoretically integrates the substantive theories on status shift developed in various contexts (transition to adulthood, professional status shifts, ageing, rites of passage in faraway cultures, initiation, soldiers returning from the front, etc.).

Even if the goal was to complete a GT journey, then, the production of a substantive theory would not represent the end. It is always possible to continue it so as to generate a general sociological theory on a significant, multi-branched category in various substantive areas (Glaser, 2007).

It is also possible, and in fact desirable, however, for researchers to return to their theories after writing their final reports in order to identify one or more research directions that were inadequately developed or intentionally discarded at the moment of outlining the theory, and expand on the further processes implied in these underdeveloped or discarded lines of inquiry.

To Sum Up

- The GT journey follows a well-marked path. It is open to the unexpected, it welcomes chaos, it is in no hurry to conceptualize and it remains faithful to the experience. By contrast, all methodological procedures are necessarily rigid and prescriptive at the moment in which they seek to freeze methodological stages and rigidly prescribe their procedures.
- Despite the due cautions and necessary distinctions, this chapter has outlined a nine-stage path in order to offer an overview of the temporal and logical sequence of GT procedures as a whole. In the following chapters, each of the main phases of the operative project of doing GT will be scrutinized in more detail and with a more demanding critical eye.

Further Readings

For the research presented here, see Tarozzi, M. (2007). *Il governo della TV. Etnografie del consumo televisivo in contesti domestici*. Milano: Franco Angeli. Especially chapter 1 *Storia di una ricerca*.

Please refer to the chapters that correspond to the various steps of the process.

Part II

Doing GT

4 Starting the Research

4.1 When to Use GT

GT is one qualitative research method among many. There is no legitimate reason to attribute to it primacy over other methods or hold it up as the exemplification of empirical research. Some scholars do tend to emphasize the original elements or typical features of GT, even to the point of distinguishing it from other qualitative methods (Glaser, 2004); this position assumes that lumping together the two approaches, descriptive and conceptual, would undermine the conceptual power of GT. As with any other qualitative research methodology, however, the scope of GT's originality is not absolute; rather, it lies in this method's particular efficacy in investigating specific objects. In functional terms, every methodology is suited to investigating certain themes according to a given perspective (Morse & Richards, 2002; Creswell, 2007).

As this chapter will show, adopting one paradigm rather than another does unquestionably impact the researcher's choice of methodology. However, this choice also depends on the *type of object* the researcher intends to investigate and, especially, the *type of gaze* he or she intends to apply to the given theme. Ultimately, the choice of research methodology depends less on the epistemological positioning and more on the nature of the research question. Therefore, researchers do not choose a methodology because they 'like it better' or 'know it better', or even because it is 'more similar' to their world view or theoretical or ideological convictions. A methodology is preferable over others because it is better suited to exploring the research question formulated for interrogating the phenomenon under investigation.

Following this pragmatic approach to choosing a methodology, what options does a qualitative researcher have for analysing a specific research question? In other words, what is the menu of handy choices for those looking to conduct qualitative research?

There are certainly many possibilities. Qualitative research undoubtedly offers a number of methodological approaches, and every qualitative research textbook suggests different taxonomies for organizing these possible approaches. Table 2 outlines some of the schemes formulated by some classical methodological studies in various disciplines (Creswell, 2007).

Considering Table 2 in a schematic way, it is clear that, despite varying premises, some traditions (highlighted in bold) appear again and again and some tendencies stand out. Following Morse and Richards (2002) and Creswell (2007), being aware of the risk of reductionism, I agree that the three main families of qualitative methodology can be identified as ethnography, phenomenology and GT. Each of these displays substantial differences in terms of theoretical premises, researcher's epistemic outlook, how the research question is formulated, type of data and collection methods and modes of analysis.

Table 2 Some Classifications of Qualitative Approaches

Qualitative Approaches		**Authors**	**Discipline/ Field**
Anthropological Perspectives Sociological Perspectives Biological Perspectives	Case Studies Personal Accounts Cognitive Studies Historical Inquiries	Lancy (1993)	Education
Grounded Theory **Ethnography**	**Phenomenology** Life Histories Conversational Analysis	Strauss & Corbin (1990)	Sociology, Nursing
Phenomenology **Ethnography**	Ethnoscience **Grounded Theory**	Morse (1994)	Nursing
Ethnography **Grounded Theory** Hermeneutics	Empirical **Phenomenological** Research Heuristic Research Transcendental **Phenomenology**	Moustakas (1994)	Psychology
Case Studies **Ethnography** **Phenomenology** Ethnomethodology	Interpretative Practices **Grounded Theory** Biographical Historical Clinical Research	Denzin & Lincoln (1994)	Social Sciences

Source: Author's reformulation of Creswell (2007).

Ethnography, developed from the research practices of cultural anthropologists, focuses on exploring the *culture* of human groups. The characteristics of these cultures are embedded in human groups and, most of the time, are tacit and implicit. As such they are more visible to an external observer (with an *etic* perspective), an outsider who seeks to summarize the insiders' (*emic*) perspective through a unitary narrative.

Phenomenology (here understood as a research methodology) derives from the philosophical tradition of phenomenology pioneered by Edmund Husserl. Phenomenology is a method for describing the lived experience of subjects in a reflexive and interpretative way; it seeks to identify their *essence*. According to this perspective, people are embodied in the world, and their perceptions of reality take a concrete form in their lived experiences. It is this fact that makes their existence meaningful and elevates it to the status of significant research object.

As the table shows, GT does not have its own univocal theoretical framework, but it does have distinct theoretical referents. Nevertheless, it shares with symbolic interactionism the view that social reality is continuously mutable, understanding such reality as the product of continuously negotiated, symbolic and intentional exchanges among people.

These fundamentally different theoretic-epistemological premises give rise to different epistemic outlooks on the part of researchers and different research techniques. The key point here, however, is that they also generate different ways of interrogating reality, different perspectives that lead researchers to select certain research themes rather than others, and different ways to formulate wholly different research questions about them.

Namely, ethnography aims to achieve 'thick description', as it was first defined in 1973 by Clifford Geertz (2017), of cultures and groups; phenomenology is aimed at exploring lived experience and the ways in which subjects grant sense to their context (aiming, or not, at grasping its essence); GT, as we have seen, seeks to identify the social processes underlying phenomena, pursuing an interpretative theory capable of integrating, synthesizing and conceptualizing empirical data. Therefore, the choice of GT is appropriate if the intention is to investigate a limited number of topics with the aim of allowing the participants or observed phenomena's underlying processes to emerge. If, instead, the intention is to describe a setting or explore the lived experiences of certain subjects in depth, it would make sense to choose the most appropriate methodologies for these aims, namely ethnography or phenomenology, respectively.

Table 3 Table Comparing the Main Qualitative Research Traditions

Methodology	Assumptions	Purpose	Methods
Ethnography	Cultural anthropology. Characteristics of a culture are embedded in a human group and are mostly tacit and implicit.	To describe the culture of a group using their symbolic system. Thick description. *How this group …* *What patterns …*	Participant observation. Field work. Interview with key informants.
Grounded theory	Sociology. Symbolic interactionism and Chicago school. Post-positivist versus constructivist tradition.	To generate a theory interpreting the processes behind certain phenomena. *What's going on there …* *What processes …*	Semi-structured interview. *All is data.*
Phenomenology	Philosophy. Phenomenology. Subjects are embodied in their world; their experiences are the outward form of their perception of reality	To understand (not explain) the meaning or the essence of the lived experience. *What's the meaning of …* *How … make sense of …*	In-depth interview. Life history. Ethnomethodology.

For instance, a typical ethnographic research question might be: 'How is corporate culture transmitted through staff training?' A phenomenological one: 'What does it mean to be a therapist?' Whereas GT would ask: 'What factors influence parents' decisions to enrol their children in private schools?'

However, the three methodologies presented here in terms of their typical characteristics might also offer different perspectives for investigating the same theme; for instance, the issue of *discrimination against ethnic minorities in a certain context* (school, workplace, hospital, etc.). In an ethnographic approach, the focus will be on exploring the context and the relationships among its actors, phenomenology might investigate the lived experience of exclusion experienced by the subjects of discrimination, and GT could investigate the processes of prejudice-construction or forms of resistance to discrimination.

Rigidity is never a distinctive trait of qualitative research, and the methods are never exclusive. A deliberate mixture of the methods is thus not only acceptable, but in many cases definitely desirable. Mixed methods are sometimes a very useful design combining not only qualitative and quantitative, but also different qualitative approaches in the same overall research project. In particular, as will be shown, GT and ethnography can prove complementary in significant ways (Charmaz & Mitchell, 2001).

To mix qualitative methods, however, it is essential to first understand the specific nature of each methodology so as to avoid superficial and naïve methods slurring (Stern, 1994; Baker et al., 1992). As with cooking an excellent dish, the chef/ researcher must understand the characteristics and flavours of the various ingredients in order to combine them wisely. It is therefore important to be familiar with the prerogatives, assumptions and implications of the methodologies before combining them. Otherwise, instead of a harmonious and rigorous combination, the only result will be a muddled research design and inedible food.

In summary, it is the specific nature of the method that first suggests the identification of the theme and formulation of the research question (the first two phases of the GT process). GT is appropriate for exploring social, educational, psychological and political processes with an eye to producing conceptualizations. It may be more ambitious than other approaches in that it aims to investigate complex, and not easily delimited, areas, dynamic issues touched by an enormous quantity of variables, and to then construct a comprehensive theory capable of answering questions about the meaning of the participants' agency and providing them with useful and effective answers. It is thus especially suitable when little is known about the area of study; that is, when previous knowledge is scarce or absent. It is also highly appropriate when one of the desired outcomes is to generate theory with explanatory power, or when an inherent process is embedded in the research situation that is likely to be explicated by GTs (Birks & Mills, 2012).

4.2 Research Question and Problem

It would be reductive to imagine that it is only the nature of the problem or type of epistemic gaze the researcher intends to turn on the theme that determines the most suitable methodology for investigating it.

4.2.1 Sensitizing Concepts

Before looking at the elements that contribute to shaping a research question in GT, it is necessary to note that a GT research theme always takes the form of a *sensitizing concept* (Blumer, 1969), a notion that is particularly meaningful in GT (Bowen, 2006). Pre-existing knowledge should be included in GT as *sensitizing concepts* rather than *analytic* or *definitive* ones. *Sensitizing* means that they offer a meaningful picture of phenomena in everyday terms (Dey, 2007) instead of prescribing what there is to see within an analytic, and closed, conceptual definition. In other words, some theoretical concepts, even though they lack empirical content and are useless or even risky in a GT inquiry, can nevertheless sensitize the researcher towards certain relevant issues and phenomena in the field under analysis. Sensitizing concepts, unlike definitive ones, are not aimed at enclosing all the common elements of a type of object within a specific definition. Rather, they offer a general sense to the social investigation, a guide for approaching a theme. Instead of providing clear guidelines about what to look at, therefore, they simply provide hints about the direction in which to look. To paraphrase a Zen proverb, such concepts do not say to look at the moon, they say to look at the finger pointing upward.

Such concepts are about ways of seeing, understanding and organizing social reality that are not closed and rigid, not rooted in our disciplinary perspectives or our views of the world (Charmaz, 2006). For this reason, sensitizing concepts have been considered valid starting points for qualitative investigation and GT in particular (Glaser, 1978; Charmaz, 2006; Bowen, 2006). Moreover, for the same reasons they are also perfectly suited to label emerging concepts in the more advanced steps of GT analysis and especially theoretical coding.

In practice, it would be naïve to think that a social researcher can select a theme and produce a research question without any knowledge or any conceptual tool from their training, scientific community, personal philosophical or ideological beliefs. Yet, GT is an inductive approach that seeks to allow a theory to emerge from the data without being influenced by assumptions made in advance of systematic empirical knowledge of the phenomena under investigation. In this regard, the notion of sensitizing concepts is helpful. It allows researchers to take concepts and notions into consideration that are fundamental in their own discipline or field of experience under investigation but without using them in a rigid way to formulate other-directed hypotheses or enclose the reality inside the confines of verbal schemes. Indeed, such rigidity makes it difficult for researchers to remain 'open to the data' (Glaser, 1978), a stance which represents an essential prerequisite of GT.

4.2.2 *Identifying an Area of Investigation or a Theme*

In qualitative inquiry, choosing a research topic (or problem) and establishing a workable research question are two different but interrelated processes, and it is difficult to define which one comes first (Miles & Huberman, 1994). Researchers are always embodied in the world they wish to explore, and their stance is never neutral or separate from the world in which they live. Carving a research question out of the topic as a whole is as difficult as isolating a figure from the background.

In the practice of research, however, the transition from the first step to the second one is essential. It also represents one of the most difficult processes, especially (but not only) for novices (Silverman, 2000).

Before examining the qualitative research problems related to this act of reducing concepts, phenomena, settings and processes into a workable research question, it is interesting to see how a research theme emerges and how a research area can be deemed relevant. There are many factors that influence the choice of a topic, and the scientific community of social scientists seems to generally agree on this point. Kenneth Bailey (2008), one of the most influential scholars in social research methods, confirmed in his bestselling handbook (ed. or. 1982) that there are six main elements that influence the researcher's choice of topic:

1) sociological paradigm;
2) researcher's values;
3) degree of reactivity;
4) methodology;
5) analysis unit;
6) time.

In general, the two most important axes influencing the choice of theme and consolidating the motivations behind the research can be said to be the researcher's deep *personal interest* rooted in a solid *scientific knowledge* of a topic. These can take on various forms and be accompanied by other, secondary elements.

- *The researcher's interests.* To fuel the motivation required to carry out multiple months of GT with all the difficulties and setbacks, concerns and frustrations that such research inevitably entails, it is fundamental that researchers, especially beginners, are prepared to answer the existential question that inexorably arises sooner or later: 'What on earth am I doing this for?' Answering this pervasive question of meaning requires strong motivation, the kind that only an engaging theme or one with strong personal, ethical, cognitive or emotional involvement can give. Investigating themes of interest to others or lacking in deep, lasting and intimate involvement, in contrast, does not guarantee the same intensity or energy in terms of motivation. For instance, Glaser once declared that both he and Strauss became interested in the theme of dying in hospital due to intense personal experiences with their parents' deaths (Glaser, 1998, p. 49). On a different level, in the research on TV governance the author shared the same set of problems faced by the families studied by virtue of having a son in the target age range.

- *Having direct experience with the theme or in the area.* The researcher's own working context, as an area of direct experience, can represent an interesting site of investigation. Over time, direct experience (that of a nurse, teacher, or manager) generates knowledge and competences that can undoubtedly help in formulating the research structure and carrying out the study. Such direct involvement can also constitute a limit in GT, however, in so far as consolidated knowledge of the experience risks undermining or blocking the emergence of the unexpected or discovery of the new when such new elements encounter the usual knowledge and practices.
- *The academic and non-academic literature.* Traditionally, it is scientific competence on a topic that leads to the research theme. Such competence is demonstrated by the ability to master the academic literature in that field, but in GT such mastery assumes a delicate and controversial role that will be addressed in more detail in section 4.2.3. Not only can the academic literature provide simple stimulus for a researcher's curiosity, but it can also be mined in search of gaps, areas not yet investigated or themes that deserve further exploration. This may represent the basis for proposing new interpretations for tackling old problems or highlighting contradictions or ambiguities among multiple interpretations of the same theme (Silverman, 1993). In the case of GT, it is nevertheless particularly important that the academic expert on a given theme and its associated literature be capable of stepping back from it and tuning in to the data. This is why Glaser (1998) invites researchers to make their dependency on the literature explicit when identifying an area of investigation. He even offers

practical advice for doing so: to adopt the attitude of jury members whose judge has ordered them not to consider a certain fact when issuing the verdict, to interview oneself as if interviewing someone else or to write an article on the analysis of the literature and publish it (Glaser, 1998, p. 120).

- *The theme is assigned or suggested*. Sometimes the choice of theme is determined by a doctoral supervisor, a targeted grant or a particularly demanding funding agency. Given the aforementioned points, even when the choice of theme is imposed, it is nevertheless important for researchers to be able to carve out an exclusive space for themselves from that top-down assigned theme, a space linked to personal interests that can serve as the anchor for their own individual motivations (Strauss & Corbin, 1998).
- *Participants' main concern*. When a method hopes to produce results that function for the practitioners and are useful in their work, the participants themselves might suggest the theme by sharing with the researcher their *main concern* (Glaser, 1998). As in participatory research design, proposing a theme that coincides with a problem that concerns the stakeholders means delegating to them the task of identifying what is relevant in a certain area. Such an approach avoids the risk of entering an area of investigation with strong assumptions, preconceived hypotheses or research questions formulated in an abstract, academic context. However, in GT specifically such delegation is not the result of ideological motivations or a way of enhancing practical knowledge; rather, it is the result of specific methodological principles. In GT, it is the focus on the main concern and the ways professionals and laymen tackle that concern that quickly leads to the identification of basic social processes. After all, these are the ways through which the people operating in a certain area seek to provide responses to their main concern.

Having identified the theme or area of investigation that the researcher is personally interested in and has scientifically mastered, a theme which, first and foremost, concerns the participants, the problem becomes one of reducing it to a *workable* question.

Doctoral students are constantly being asked by their supervisors to narrow the field and to carry out that laborious and complex work of specifying the research theme in order to narrow it down to a research question, which is manageable in terms of time and allows the researcher to exercise control over the investigation processes.

Pinpointing a precise research question from a topic is not only important in that it reduces the inquiry to a workable size; it is also important in that the methods should be congruent with the research question (Baker, West, & Stern, 1992; Morse & Field, 1995). The qualitative researcher needs a clear, focused and defined question which interprets not only the theme, but also the stance and tone of the research. In reality, I only partially agree with this statement. Over time, I have noted that several elements contribute to shaping a research question, and I will outline these in the following paragraphs.

The question of transposing a theme into a research question is complex and heavily debated. The act of reducing complexity always entails two risks: simplification and one-sidedness. Both of these risks are particularly serious in a study that aims to build a theory grounded in the data. At this stage, researchers run the risk of formulating a research question that is not only manageable, clear, easy to convey to the funders or supervisor, and coherent with the literature, but also prejudiced and preconceived. Excluding the chaos from an area of investigation can also mean taking refuge in the convenient belief that there exists a superior order overseeing the complexity of reality and considering this to be the object of scientific knowledge.

No reduction is ever neutral. The act of *a priori* formulating a proposition that defines the phenomenon to be investigated in detail implies a reduction of the field of experience that inhibits, or even nullifies, the construction of a theory grounded in the data. Indeed, it was this point that represented one of the main divergences between the two founders of GT (Glaser, 1992, chap. 4). Strauss and Corbin (1990) argued that it was desirable and necessary to formulate a research question that allowed the researcher to make the general research problem viable in order to establish its borders and thus determine, *a priori*, what is and is not relevant to the study. Glaser argued that this operation, carried out before accessing the field, was inappropriate and unsatisfactory; instead, he asserted, researchers need to go to the field after having identified an area of investigation but without a precise research question in mind. Once there, they must allow the participants' main concern to emerge, so as to examine how it might be managed and then use it to identify the underlying social processes. For instance, in the first pioneering study on the awareness of dying in hospital, the two authors did not know *a priori* that the analysis of those settings would lead them to investigate the notion of 'awareness'. They went into hospital departments where death was frequent (intensive care, oncology, emergency etc.) to see what happened. Only afterwards, following immersion in the field, did they perceive the central problem, a problem of intense concern to the hospital staff, namely that of generating contexts of awareness.

Therefore, the general research question for starting GT research is synthesized well by the oft-repeated motto, 'What's going on here?' (Glaser, 1978). A more focused question arises afterwards; the researcher specifies it as part of analysis and the question in turn guides the theoretical sampling.

4.2.3 *Formulating a Research Question*

Glaser's warnings are important for fully understanding the nature of the method and avoiding the trap of forcing the data to lead the researcher within a manageable, but inevitably reductive and preconceived, research question. Nevertheless, in actual research practice it is important that data collection be accompanied by the attempt to formulate questions that are gradually more precise, so as to better comprehend the specific object of the investigation. In this sense, the strategies suggested by Strauss and Corbin (especially 1998) are also useful devices that can help GT users, especially beginners, in the process of data collection. In fact, making an effort to define the research question helps to narrow the theme, that is, to identify the most relevant aspects of the area of investigation.

The following are examples of research questions formulated in a typical GT style: what processes do certain typologies of brand-consumer relationships create in certain life conditions? (Fournier, 1998); what impact does a certain school have on the learning of students at risk of school failure? (Pressley et al., 2006); what are the barriers to consistent condom use and different coping strategies among female sex workers in China? (Choi & Holroyd, 2007); what are the emotional experiences of teenagers and young adults with suicidal experiences and how do they respond to their emotional states? (Everall, Bostik, & Paulson, 2006); and, how do high-performing companies in the fashion industry coordinate their supply chain activities? (Bowon, 2013).

Broadly speaking, various elements converge in suggesting the formulation of the research question, both at the beginning and in its progressively more focused versions during the process. These elements appear as constraints that delimit the borders of the area of investigation within which the research process unfolds. There are a few elements which simply cannot be ignored in formulating the research, as outlined here.

The constraints of the paradigm. The research paradigm the researcher adopts is not limited to providing an idea of science and scientific knowledge at the epistemological level that is accepted by a certain scientific community. Not only do paradigms distinguish between 'normal science' (Kuhn, 1996) and deviations from such science, they also determine what problems or questions are important for a given scientific community and define the theories, methods and techniques considered acceptable. Paradigms thus inform the gaze of the researcher, influencing his or her way of looking at reality and ability to question it. A paradigm is the window through which the researcher sees the world and it performs and elicits the questions that are worth investigating (Kuhn, 1996). Paradigms frame the theme and question in a suitable way while imposing a certain stance on researchers by shaping the way they interrogate reality and select some objects instead of others. In so doing, paradigms define the problems, issues, objects and methods to be addressed. Over the last few decades, many scholars have argued about how many such paradigms exist and what they should be called. However, the important point here is that placing a researchable question within a positivistic or constructivist paradigm will radically transform the research question itself. That is why conceptions of reality, conceptualizations of the relationship between researchers and their subjects and participants, and the methods and techniques considered appropriate and acceptable vary at a fundamental level.

Therefore, the possibility of interrogating reality with a focused research question and refining and shaping a general theme is intimately related to the kind of knowledge that the researcher expects to discover or construct, and to the question of how this is considered achievable. These constraints work, often unconsciously, to distinguish different ways of defining the research question, including among the various 'schools' of GT.

Constraints imposed by the funding bodies. It is very common to overlook the politics of the research and how they impact the research design (Cheek, 2000, 2005). Research completely free of politics is not possible in either the realm of pure research or that of applied work. According to the traditional distinction between pure (or basic) and applied (which is not actually appropriate in the case of GT) research, pure research involves developing and verifying theories and hypotheses that are intellectually interesting for the researcher rather than by virtue of their concrete applications (Bailey, 2008), whereas applied research is usually linked to resolving practical problems and, hence, often funded by private or public bodies that expect concrete and visible results. All funding is accompanied by an expectation that the research will produce outcomes, a certain political will and adherence to a social discourse that has an impact on the way the research question is formulated. The nature of this 'political' impact should not be taken for granted. Moreover, researchers should not underestimate the consequences that negotiations with the funder will have on the methodological level, a fact which requires the ability to manage such consequences at the political level (Tarozzi, 2013).

Can research ever be unfunded, however, in the sense of being completely independent, guided only by the researcher? While there are different ways to fund research in different countries, both public and private funding always conditions and shapes the scope, range and purpose of the research question; the researcher is never entirely free to develop the aims of the study or its general direction. As Julianne Cheek has noted, seeking, 'gaining and accepting funding for qualitative research is not a neutral, value-free process' (Cheek, 2005, p. 387).

The constraints of the researcher. The very act of adopting one paradigm or another is never ethically neutral, and the same applies to methodological choices. The choice of the research question is affected by ethical constraints as well as the ideological, religious, political and moral beliefs of the researcher which lead to formulating the question in a way that is not neutral or objective. Researchers' values direct their view towards a *must be* and entail value judgements regarding the reality to be investigated that extend beyond the empirical investigation. The example research mentioned earlier regarding discrimination against ethnic minorities in organizational contexts (schools, hospitals, companies) starts from an ideological assumption, linked to the researcher's values, that discrimination exists and that it constitutes a force which must be combatted. Facing such a reality, two paths loom before the researcher. One is to chase the myth of value-free social research in which researchers disassociate themselves from their values and act as if it were possible to be ethically detached from their subject of investigation and to regard it with a cold, objective and neutral gaze. If, as I believe, this is neither possible nor desirable, the second is to begin by acknowledging the impossibility of this disassociation. Researchers who are aware of their own values clarify their own impact on the reality that they are going to investigate. Therefore, rather than chasing some impossible ethical neutrality, the task is to not take for granted even the elements that derive from the value judgements influencing the choice of the area of investigation and formulation of the research question, and instead to thoughtfully analyse such elements.

Organizational constraints. Besides the factors mentioned earlier, there are also organizational constraints that condition the formulation itself of the research question and accompany the process of reducing the complexity of the theme. These constraints have to do with the availability of resources, amount of time available, difficulty of access the field and ability to recruit participants. All of these constraints end up having a direct impact on the way researchers circumscribe the research question and, later on, delimit the theory. It is wise to predict such constraints; however, the kind of forethought and efficiency-oriented, instrumental rationality that makes choices based solely on cost-benefit analysis cannot be the only, nor perhaps the main, element determining how research questions investigating the social, psychological, educational or political themes we find exciting are formulated.

4.2.4 Academic Literature

Unlike mainstream social research involving a systematic analysis of the relevant academic literature *before* starting an empirical study, GT has since its founding text suggested diving immediately into the field to collect and analyse the data. For Barney Glaser (1978, 1992, 1998), this is more than just a reasonable suggestion for an inductive method; in GT, it is a 'very strong dictum': 'do not do a literature review in the substantive area and related areas where research has to be done' (Glaser, 1998, p. 67). Some recent scholars of classic GT such as Holton (2007) have also echoed this admonition.

The general logic behind this provocatory and controversial dictum is comprehensible and, all in all, coherent with the method itself. In research aimed at building a theory beginning from the data, any analysis of the preliminary literature would generate certain preconceptions, thus potentially inhibiting the emergence of insights and the formulation of original categories based on this specific experience.

Nonetheless, despite its comprehensibility and consistency with the method, critics have taken issue in particular with the implicit anti-academic and anti-scientific attitude underlying such a guideline. Many have criticized this position or have instead argued for the exact opposite, namely using the existing literature in the substantive field as part of constructivist GT (Thornberg, 2012; Thornberg & Dunne, 2019). Delaying the literature review until the end of analysis has been regarded as ingenuous, unscientific and impracticable. The assumption that the researcher should adopt an objective and neutral position as if he or she were a *tabula rasa* is naïve (Dey, 2007); in reality, such an approach is not feasible in an academic context in which research committees, funding bodies and ethics committees understandably expect research proposals to include a critical engagement with the relevant literature in the field (Bryant, 2017). What is more, a theory generated through GT that does not engage the current debate on the theme is likely to be extremely superficial, say predictable things or even 'reinvent the wheel' (Silverman, 2000).

As is often the case with founders' most extreme positions, it is key to comprehend the reasons behind this operational prescription and then take it with a grain of salt.

Even wishing to do so, moreover, it would be impossible for a doctoral student to ignore the scientific literature on the theme because the board of examiners would never approve a thesis without an analysis of the literature, nor would it be possible to have a grant application or article in a peer-reviewed journal accepted.

Instead, it is important to conduct a wide-ranging critical analysis of the literature. As long as it is not limited to a show of erudition or composite text resembling a reasoned bibliography, this serves to render a more dense theoretical argument and increases the credibility of the research (Charmaz, 2006). Like a GT itself, the analysis of the literature is expressed in an analytical rather descriptive form, critically conceptualizing the contributions of each carefully selected source and combining them into an argument. The resulting text does not necessarily need to be positioned at the beginning of an article, volume or thesis, however. In fact, besides the literature review conducted in the early stages of the research process, in GT it is highly valuable to return to the literature in the later stages of the process (Bryant, 2017). Throughout the process, researchers should seek to bring their findings from the library into dialogue with their findings from the field, to encourage the emerging theory to find a position, to reveal its limitations, to discuss its significance and to highlight gaps in the existing literature.

4.3 Ethics

By now it is consolidated practice to have a research project approved by an ethics committee or Institutional Review Board (IRB) or make it consistent with to a specific ethical code. Beyond institutional obligations, however, even though adhering to an ethical code can seem an annoying if unavoidable waste of time, attention to research ethics is fundamental and holds a more and more central place in discussions of qualitative research (Flick, 2018). Classic GT works do not mention ethical issues. This is due in part to a historical difference in the awareness of ethical questions; unlike the late 1960s, such issues are currently imperative in every research project. In particular, ethics are inextricable from the very idea of qualitative research and constitutively connected with doing GT when engaging subjects and asking them to dedicate their time to participate in a study. GT deals mostly with concepts, so there are generally no risks to the subjects' physical well-being; however, it is necessary to scrupulously guarantee their anonymity and some caution is necessary, especially when asking them to refer to painful aspects of their lives.

While Ethics Committee approval is a common requirement for all types of research, in GT there are peculiar difficulties but also some particular resources (Glaser, 2001, p. 128). For instance, it is impossible to define in advance the exact size of the sample or what types of subjects will take part in the study; the GT researcher cannot predict exactly what features that they will need to have, how they will be located or where the data collection will proceed, since the subjects will naturally be located according to the logic of theoretical sampling, and this sampling gradually increases as the theory is developed. One practical suggestion as mentioned in Chapter 3 is to overestimate the size of all data collection elements (number of participants, interview questions, timing) or to identify a range for possible number of participants and research units so as to avoid having to resubmit the proposal for amendments.

GT has also some strengths on the ethical level, however. The participants are naturally more interested in the study than with some other approaches, seeing as the researcher starts from their 'main concern' and develops outcomes that will have a practical impact on the context under investigation and promote social change. The participants are acknowledged in their full dignity as human beings in that they are valued for their professionalism and, in part, called on to actively cooperate in constructing the research. In this sense, they are not affected by the guinea pig syndrome plaguing most social research studies or even many medical ones, which often treat subjects as passive and anonymous providers of data. Another strength of GT, from a research ethics point of view, is that producing theorizations rather than descriptions is more effective than other descriptive qualitative studies at safeguarding participants' anonymity and privacy. GT reports usually include few direct references to the subjects (besides some rare citations which can easily be rendered anonymous). Instead, the GT user employs conceptualizations of processes that are not directly referable to the subjects whose discursive formulation and observed actions have produced them.

4.4 Collecting and Constructing Data

GT does not provide specific indications about collecting data and may take advantage of many different sources of data. Since it is considered, above all, a method for analysing qualitative data, its originality lies mainly in analytical practices. Due to this emphasis on theory building and associated limited attention to data collection, GT has sometimes been accused of excessively accelerating the construction of schemes (Lofland & Lofland, 1984) while underestimating the importance of the construction of data. This is particularly evident in Glaser & Strauss's initial *Discovery*, where the authors refer to data collection in terms of the logical process for locating relevant information but do not focus on how to collect this information as data (Flick, 2018).

Recently, however, scholars have dedicated more attention to reflecting methodologically on the type of data appropriate for building a GT and methods for collecting them (Charmaz, 2001, 2014). Although there is a tendency to privilege verbal data collected through interviews, there are various types of data, all rich and useful, that can be usefully collected to build a good GT; such an approach reflects Glaser's motto according to which, in GT, 'all is data' (Glaser, 2001, chap. 11). For instance, lately scholars have granted particular attention to the use of visual data in GT (Konecki, 2011; Mey & Dietrich, 2016) or, more recently, big data (Bryant, 2017). For the sake of brevity, the following overview refers to three main tools that assume particular characteristics in GT and that somehow encompass the use of other data collection techniques:

- observation;
- interviewing;
- document and textual analysis.

4.4.1 Observation

This tool, especially understood as an ethnographic device, allows researchers to record participants' behaviours in their environment, community or social context. The aim of this tool is to capture the perspective of the insiders even while remaining an outsider by combining the two types of viewpoint, *emic* and *etic*.

The specificity of ethnographic observation in GT is that, from the outset, it aims to observe the phenomena, and especially the elements of process, defined in the research question rather than dwelling on a description of the context. Therefore, such observation becomes gradually more focused and always seeks to produce conceptualizations of the processes under examination rather than detailed descriptions. This also prevents the risk, typical of all ethnography, of gathering loads of diverse data because everything seems equally relevant and nothing secondary; the resulting issue is that researchers then produce data from which it is very difficult to extract interpretative categories or integrate categories among each other. Observers in this case are not passive receivers of objective data. Even while remaining faithful to the phenomenon, they direct their gaze at episodes, space and time which are linked to the main concern of the participants and basic social process so as to grasp the central categories of the emerging theory. As shown, this is made possible by the fact that observation proceeds hand in hand with analysis and the latter periodically redirects the observational gaze, focusing and clarifying it.

Charmaz and Mitchell (2001, see also Charmaz, 2014) have delved particularly deeply into the relationship between ethnography and GT, and they suggest some guiding questions that can help in 'reading' the setting and allowing the meanings the participants give to their own actions to rise to the surface. These guiding questions should not be taken as a grid that structures observations, as such observations must always remain open-ended. Rather, the questions can represent an open check-list serving as a useful tool for launching the observation (Charmaz & Mitchell, 2001, p. 163):

- What is the setting of action? When and how does action take place?
- What is going on? What is the overall activity being studied, the relatively long-term behaviour about which participants organize themselves? What specific acts comprise this activity?
- What is the distribution of participants over space and time in these locales?
- How are actors organized? How do organizations effect, oversee, regulate or promote this activity?
- How are members stratified? Who is ostensibly in charge? Does being in charge vary by activity? How is membership achieved and maintained?
- What do actors pay attention to? What is important, preoccupying and critical?
- What do they pointedly ignore that other persons might pay attention to?
- What symbols do actors invoke to understand their worlds, the participants and processes within them, and the objects and events they encounter? What names do they attach to objects, events, persons, roles, settings and equipment?
- What practices, skills, stratagems and methods of operation do actors employ?
- Which theories, motives, excuses, justifications or other explanations do actors use in accounting for their participation? How do they explain to each other, not to outside investigators, what they do and why they do it?
- What goals do actors seek? When, from their perspective, is an act well or poorly done? How do they judge action – by what standards, developed and applied by whom?
- What rewards do various actors gain from their participation?

In recording observational data, it is important to try to keep description distinct from interpretation, the facts and the meaning-making regarding those facts. According to a radically constructivist research paradigm, the descriptive and interpretative levels cannot possibly be distinguished. According to the phenomenological perspective I endorse, however, it is important to pursue this distinction as much as possible and to value the exercise of describing phenomena as faithfully as possible. To achieve this aim, it can be useful to

Table 4 Example of Descriptive and Interpretive Field Notes

Descriptive notes *What's happening?*	**Interpretive or reflective notes** *What does it mean?*

divide field notes into two separate areas, with notes of descriptions (what happens) in one part and interpretations (what it means) in another (Table 4). These are both important and actually intertwined; however, in order to grant value to their heuristic contribution it is important to be able to maintain them as separate and reflect on their correlations afterwards.

4.4.2 *Interviewing*

The interview is one of the main tools featured in the qualitative research approaches (Gubrium & Holstein, 2001), and in GT it assumes some specific features (Charmaz, 2014, chap 4). GT interviews are conversations with the goal of enabling the in-depth exploration of a certain theme; what they seek to bring to the surface is the way participants make sense of their own experiences. Interviews are thus not tools for collecting 'facts' but rather a way to generate interpretations of experiences, always positioning such statements in the context that generated them.

Verbal data from the participants are the data that best express what is important to them. Such data provide a direct account of the processes under way. Moreover, through semi-structured interviews researchers can calibrate the questions by following the course of theoretical sampling and by formulating questions which become gradually more focused as the theory emerges and the research field narrows around the core category.

The interview is directed at exploring the basic social process and the ways through which the participants' experiences deliberately fit into that process. The aim is to stimulate participants' reflection on the basis of personal experiences as opposed to theoretical or ideological beliefs. The most appropriate way to do so is in-depth interviewing that explores but does not interrogate. Such interviewing should leave a certain space open for interviewees' digressions but also remain sufficiently focused on the theme the interviewer wants to explore and to which he or she constantly returns. This is the type of *intensive interviewing* that Kathy Charmaz has theorized (2014) as the in-depth exploration of a particular topic with a subject who has had relevant experience. Such in-depth exploration of participants' experience with the research topic calls for a sympathetic stance on the part of the researcher, based on open-ended questions posed to carefully selected, key informants possessed of substantial experience.

Certainly, the various schools of GT have suggested different ways of posing questions, according to the epistemological paradigm underlying the method. Objectivist GT is thus especially interested in allowing the facts, temporal sequences, behaviours and incidents to emerge, whereas constructivist GT will attempt to capture the meaning of those facts and incidents by asking respondents to define and explain what they mean. Such an approach allows the meanings, implicit assumptions and tacit rules that guide behaviours and give meaning to events to rise to the surface.

Interviewers as grounded theorists run two major risks in conducting interviews: *asking superficial questions* that do not allow the interviewee to reveal the meaning of their own experience; and *asking questions that force and induce the answers* and impose their view and that of the subject. It is fundamental that these risks be reduced. Let us not forget that, if they provide poor data, even the largest number of interviews will not lend themselves to the process of abstracting concepts and categories from them. Rather than the quantity of interviews, it is their significance and the richness of the data that make the analysis agile and theoretically powerful. Therefore, *planning* and *listening* are essential: accurately planning the questions, asking them in a careful manner, being open and flexible and remaining in the relationship with participants. In order to strike that very difficult balance between asking meaningful questions and avoiding caging the answers to them within one's own concepts, assumptions and preconceptions, it is fundamental that researchers maintain a reflective attitude and adjust their language to that of respondents. At the basis of this entire task is the capacity to listen. Active, careful, non-judgemental and empathic listening is required, and such a stance can be achieved by always showing that what the interviewees are saying is important, interesting and pleasant; this makes people feel comfortable and facilitates the verbalization of their experiences. Given the importance of the relationship, it is preferable to conduct 'intensive' interviews, possibly repeated, rather than one-shot interviews.

As for the type of question, some examples in a GT context are presented here (see box), divided into opening, intermediate and concluding questions, drawn mainly from Charmaz (2014). Some examples actual of questions are also presented, and these are from the research chosen to exemplify the GT process in the previous chapter. In general, it can be argued that open, strongly evocative questions are preferable in GT; the kind of questions that require broad answers (especially in the first phases) but, at the same time, are well anchored in the person's own experience.

1) *Opening Questions*

(Initial or relational, open, questions to break the ice. Descriptive and not very invasive questions can be used which, only in this phase, also lead to statements)

Tell me about what happened (or how you came to__________)

Tell me what's going on when your child asks to watch TV?

When, if at all, did you first experience ____________ or notice _________

Could you describe the events that led up to_____________?

When did you first feel the need to control TV use? Can you describe everything that pushed you to this?

How do you describe the person you were then?

Can you describe what used to happen, on an ordinary day, around eight pm when you were a child?

Now can you describe what happens today on an ordinary day at the same time?

2) *Intermediate Questions*

(Structural: they show how subjects organize their knowledge; in contrast: regarding the meaning attributed to situations through comparison; projective: they invite the interviewee to imagine an ideal situation in which a certain incident can be placed)

Could you tell me about your thoughts and your feelings when you first learnt to____________?
Could you tell me about how you learnt to handle____________?

What positive/ negative changes (if any) have occurred in your life since______

What do you think are the best ways to handle a good use of TV? How did you discover or invent them?
What helps you to manage TV? What problems do you encounter with this? What are the origins of these problems?
When have you happened to think, in reference to your child's TV experience: 'Here, this thing or this situation are really appropriate for my child'?
How did it happen? What elements influenced your judgement?
Could I ask you to describe the most important lessons you learnt through experiencing_________?
How have your TV opinions and your habits changed, if they have, since you've had a child?

Where do you see yourself in two years [five years, ten years, as appropriate]? Describe the person you hope to be then. How would you compare the person you hope to be and the person you see yourself as now?

3) *Concluding Questions*

What do you think are the most important ways to _____________? How did you discover them?

How have you grown as a person since_____________? Tell me about the strengths you discovered or developed through_______________
What do you most value about yourself now? What do others most value in you?

Do you feel better as a parent since you found ways to manage TV?
What do you especially appreciate in yourself from this point of view?

Is there something that you might not have thought about before that occurred to you during this interview?
In the light of your experiences, what advice would you give to a new parent who is about to face the same situation?

Is there anything you would like to add? Is there anything you would like to ask me?

4.4.2.1 *Recording*

The recommendation of classic, Glaserian GT is to *not* record interviews (Glaser, 1998). Despite this suggestion, it is actually highly advisable to record and faithfully transcribe the interviews. Glaser's advice, while definitely divergent from current approaches in qualitative research, does have some reasons behind it, however. In fact, Glaser (1998) asserts that, since the aim of the interviews is to obtain not an accurate description but the conceptualization of the data, the use of a recorder does not in any way foster the production of concepts and categories; instead, it encourages researchers to search for descriptive completeness and a mirroring correspondence to the data that undermines the power of the GT method. For instance, according to Glaser, transcribing slows down the coding work that needs to happen together with the data collection and it provides an enormous quantity of unnecessary data. Instead, it would be enough to write some quick field notes after the interview recording what emerged from the interview.

I understand the reasons behind this methodological guideline (*cardinal rule*, ivi, p. 107) from classic GT and even partly agree with Glaser's argument that directing the mind towards description inhibits and neutralizes the act of abstraction, the *insight* necessary to elevate the level of theorization in order to codify the data. However, anyone who wants to do research seriously must remain faithful to the phenomenon. The problem is not the lack of objectivity involved in a subjective account of an interview, as any myth of objectivity has long been abandoned. What is essential, rather, is remaining faithful to the phenomenon, having respect for the hidden contours of things and authentically listening for the phenomenon as it manifests itself, even if doing so requires more efforts of conceptualizing. More concretely, recording and transcribing is what allows the researcher to:

- remain as close as possible to the participants' words;
- grasp nuances that can be particularly revealing;
- have auto-reflective feedback on the way interviews are being conducted and the relationship managed;
- remain wholly in the relationship during the conversation, without worrying about remembering or taking notes.

4.4.3 *Document and Textual Analysis*

Besides observations and interviews, there are many other sources of useful data for building a GT. Of these, documentary and textual data undoubtedly stand out. Even as early as the later 1960s the founders of GT encouraged practitioners to pursue new sources of qualitative data (Glaser & Strauss, 1967, chap. VII) such as documents, archives, newspapers, images or even the library itself; with some cautions, a library can serve as a field in which to interrogate books as if they were research participants.

Charmaz makes the useful distinction (2006) that documents can be *elicited* or *pre-extant* texts. Elicited texts are those that involve the participants in the production of written data, such as open-ended questionnaires or, more appropriately, autobiographical accounts, life stories or diaries solicited by the researcher. Extant texts occur independent of the researcher's requests and include letters, grey material, reports, projects, discussion forums on the internet, literature and published autobiographies.

This type of data can be usefully compared with data from the field, thus revealing divergences between actions and accounts of them. This strategy was used in research on the integration practices of foreign students in northern Italian schools, for instance. In this study, a comparison between statements made during the interviews, direct observation in the classroom and materials documenting the activity showed a gap between the declared intercultural integration approach and concrete practices, which did not actually follow the official model (Tarozzi, 2006).

In relation to pre-extant texts, do not make the mistake of considering them objective data. Each text is always linked to a specific occasion; it has its own specific recipients, a communicative style linked to the occasion and a communicative intent that must be acknowledged. Rarely can secondary data suited for textual analysis be considered sufficient to conduct an analysis. Unlike interviews or observations that gradually become more and more focused, these extant texts are fixed data that cannot be modulated by using the theoretical sampling process. Therefore, they are mostly complementary to observations or interviews. Alternately, they may constitute useful stimuli for conducting interviews in which, starting from texts (elicited or pre-extant), participants are asked to explicate the meaning of the statements expressed there.

To Sum Up

- Reasons for using GT rather than other methods are mostly determined by the nature of the problem to be investigated and by the type of gaze the researcher intends to turn on it. A unique feature of GT, unlike other approaches, lies in its ability to explore processes.

- The task of identifying an area of investigation is always located in the intersection of two main axes: personal interest and academic competence; in GT, these axes are also accompanied by attention to the main concern expressed by the actors in a certain context.
- Translating a theme into a research question is a necessary but delicate process in which it risks reduction and simplification along preconceived lines.
- Having outlined the old dispute about the use of scientific literature in GT and the ethical implications of the latter, various data collection techniques are addressed, critically presented in terms of three overall groups: ethnographic observation, interviewing and document analysis. Each of these assumes a peculiar form in GT and displays specific shortcomings and strengths; these were examined in light of practical indications and examples.

Further Reading

On Sensitizing Concepts

Bowen, G. A. (2006). Grounded Theory and Sensitizing Concepts. *International Journal of Qualitative Methods*, 5 (3), Article 2.

Van den Hoonard, W. C. (1997). *Working with Sensitizing Concepts: Analytical Field Research*. London: Sage.

On Various Methodological Approaches

Morse, J. M. (2001). Situating Grounded Theory within Qualitative Inquiry. In R. S. Schreiber, & Ph. N. Stern (Eds.), *Using Grounded Theory in Nursing*. New York: Springer, 1–15.

Morse, J., & Richards, L. (2002). *Readme First: For a User's Guide to Qualitative Methods*. Thousand Oaks, CA: Sage (second edition Richards & Morse, 2007).

Creswell, J. (2007). *Qualitative Inquiry and Research Design: Choosing among Five Traditions*, II ed. Thousand Oaks, CA: Sage.

Wertz, F. J. (2011). *Five Ways of Doing Qualitative Analysis: Phenomenological Psychology, Grounded Theory, Discourse Analysis, Narrative Research, and Intuitive Inquiry*. New York: Guilford Press.

On Data Collection

Flick, J. U. (2018). *The Sage Handbook of Qualitative Data Collection*. Los Angeles: Sage.

Gubrium J. F., & Holstein J. A. (Eds.) (2001). *Handbook of Interview Research: Context and Method*. Thousand Oaks, CA: Sage.

Kvale, S., & Brinkmann, S. (2015). *Interviews: Learning the Craft of Qualitative Research Interviewing*, 3rd edn. Thousand Oaks, CA: Sage Publications.

Crow, G., & Edwards, R. (2013). *What Is Qualitative Interviewing?* London: Bloomsbury Publishing.

Coffey, A. (2014). Analysing Documents in Flick. In U. Flick (Ed.), *The SAGE Handbook of Qualitative Data Analysis*. Los Angeles: Sage, 367–79.

On Ethics

Wiles, R. (2012). *What Are Qualitative Research Ethics?* London: Bloomsbury Academic.

5 Analysis: The Conceptual Work of Coding

5.1 Three Levels of Coding

Analysis in GT is a complex but structured process arranged around three progressive moments of conceptual coding; beginning from these moments, it integrates the categories that have emerged from coding and the researcher's reflections made during the course of formulating the categories into a coherent theory. Moreover, memoing and diagramming are also additional key interpretive procedures for GT analysis. For clarity, this chapter focuses on the coding process while the Chapter 6 discusses interpretive procedures, but in reality both of these dimensions of analysis are closely intertwined.

Coding in particular can be regarded as an analytical process located at the intersection between data collection and the theory produced by the GT user to account for the data. Mainly, coding is *the set of procedures and techniques to conceptualize the data*. Coding is more of an analytical than interpretative process. It abstracts concepts from the data to give rise to an interpretation that is well anchored and rooted in the data.

As suggested in the description of the global process of GT, coding occurs in three progressive phases, each one conceptually higher than the last. The first of these, *initial coding*, explores the data analytically, opening them up in all possible directions of meaning by meticulously and in detail investigating each portion of text constituting the data and assigning the first conceptual labels or codes. The second, *focused coding*, analyses the shared conceptual elements underlying wider portions of text. At the same time, it also organizes and synthesizes the data by drafting categories and grouping them into macro categories. These phases follow one another only in a conceptual sense. In fact, if analysis necessarily starts with the transcription and first 'open' reading of the data, some elements of focused coding may appear quite early and take place simultaneously because of the specific conditions of the context. For instance, such conditions might enable the researcher to develop an insight or make an analytical leap that leads him or her to define categories or their properties during the first moments of the research. In the same way, in advanced phases of the coding process it is often necessary to return to the data in an open and detailed manner. The third phase is the moment of theory building, called *theoretical coding*. When the categories are mature, the researcher highlights the connections that link them and integrates them within a coherent and unitary theory or theoretical framework explaining the phenomenon under investigation.

On closer inspection, following the logic that governs the GT process, there are two logical coding phases supporting the three practical steps listed in Figure 6. The first is more descriptive, firmly grounded in the data, aimed at developing codes that represent the basic elements for further conceptual elaboration. The techniques suggested for this phase must support the researcher in staying deeply rooted in the data, because they are like the empirical roots of the future theoretical formulations. If the roots run deep, then the theory that derives from them (the crown of the tree) will be 'grounded'. The second phase must be more conceptualizing. It should allow the researcher to take off from the descriptive level and fly up into the sky of conceptual abstraction. If the crown of the tall tree flourishes, the results will be a 'theory', a sophisticated conceptualization rooted or grounded in the data. In summary, without the latter phase the

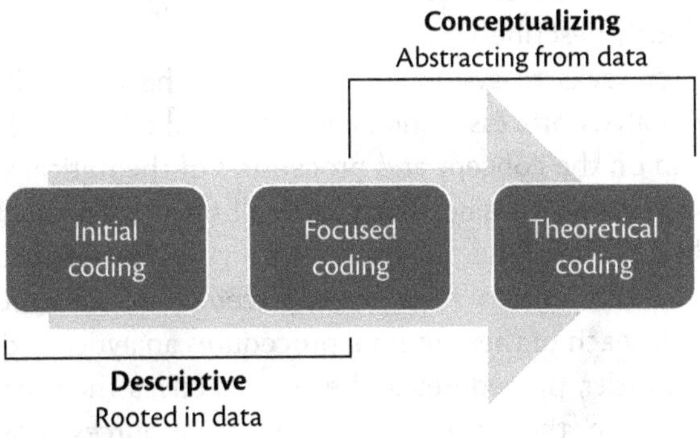

Figure 6 Three levels of coding.

results are nothing but a flat description repeating the data in other words; without the former, the results are arbitrary or ideological opinions not supported by data.

Some traditions of content analysis (see, for instance, Miles & Huberman, 1994, p. 54) apply pre-extant categories, interpretative grids given *a priori*, to analyse the data, finding recurrences and theoretically arranging them. A characteristic trait of coding in GT is that the categories are instead created beginning from the data. Nevertheless, the coding process should not be understood as a set of mechanical procedures capable of objectively grasping the ordered recurrences hiding behind the multiplicity of data. The work of coding does not unveil the functioning models of the phenomena; it does not guarantee access to the thing itself simply by coding its phenomenal manifestations or 'unearth' those latent patterns that the classic GT tradition (Glaser, 1978, 1998; and more recently Holton & Walsh, 2017) promises to achieve through an objectivist perspective. 'While the researcher codifies, analyses and extends the theoretical sampling' – Glaser writes – 'the structural models latent in the substantive theory emerge' (1998, p. 26). Indeed, the codes are not there, enclosed in the data. Rather, the task of extracting them is up to the researcher. Coding is thus closely connected to naming processes and inextricably caught up in the dimension of language. Through language, it somehow *constructs* the interpretative categories (Charmaz, 2000) that are also rooted in the phenomena which generated them. In a way, therefore, coding can always be defined as a meaning-making process, albeit never completely free or infinite. It is always linked to the constraints imposed by the data, and the interpretative work of coding unfolds within the precise boundaries set by the phenomena, accurately and meticulously described.

This chapter seeks to systematically present the three phases of the coding and analysis process – initial, focused and theoretical – followed by a follow-up on the concept and procedures of theoretical sampling. In reading this description it is necessary to recall, once again, that the process is never really as linear as it is presented here. In the interests of explanatory clarity, the various phases have been placed in an ordered temporal succession with each of their internal procedures analytically defined. The chronological order, procedures and even objectives themselves actually depend largely on the settings, constraints, resources, obstacles and 'theoretical sensitivity' (Glaser, 1978) of the researcher.

5.1.1 Initial Coding

Strauss and Corbin (1998) call the first phase of the process 'open coding'. This definition is appropriate in many ways, as defining coding as 'open' bears two meanings: on the one hand, it is open because the researcher remains open to the data, ready to welcome stimuli flowing from them; on the other hand, it is open in the sense that this type of coding is aimed at opening up or unpacking the data, at expanding fragments of text to allow all the possible meanings that the text is able to generate to come to the surface. In short, in this (and only this) phase, researchers are advised to remain very close to the data and explore every theoretical possibility stemming from them. Initial coding is thus characterized by a meticulous adherence to the participants' words or the texts just as they have been collected and coding is carried out using, as much as possible, the participants' words themselves. The aim is that of labelling each segment of data or single words to obtain 'codes'. These are neither categories nor concepts; they are the first rudimentary conceptual bricks that can be used in constructing the subsequent theoretical formulations. They need to be firmly grounded in the data because, otherwise, the subsequent theory risks being only pure, unfounded opinion. They also need to be sufficiently conceptualized, however, to summarize and account for the portion of text they refer to.

For a neophyte, this phase may seem very dispersive and at times angst-ridden. Indeed, such coding takes the initial generative question, which was already broad, and opens it up even more. The coded texts suggest countless new possible perspectives, each of which indicating unexpected lines of research, trajectories to follow, relevant themes. To do GT, however, it is imperative that researchers learn to coexist with external chaos as well as their own internal anxieties. The only flashlight illuminating the path of initial coding lies in the objectives of this phase: to elicit some concepts, expressed through categories which may not be saturated or completely developed yet.

From another viewpoint, being open to the data does not mean researchers assume they will be able to tackle the first attempt at formulating them with mind unobstructed by any kind of preconceived notions, assumptions and pre-understandings about the theme. The idea of researchers preparing to face the data in a neutral, virginal and non-judgemental manner is a myth most everyone has abandoned. Rather, it is about having an open attitude towards the data and, especially, being able to handle your own pre-understandings (Thornberg, 2012). In light of this point, a phenomenological style and certain tools formulated in that school of thought, such as the ability to bracket (suspending judgement), prove to be indispensable heuristic stances. These should be part of not only researchers' toolboxes but also and especially their posture and mentality.

The process of interview transcription is already part of coding. It is an interpretative task that entails reducing complex communication into a single verbal, linguistic code. Such reduction always takes place on multiple communicative levels (linguistic, paralinguistic, proxemics, kinaesthetic, sociocultural, etc.). In order to respect the phenomenon, however, the goal is the most accuracy possible and a rigorous description of the experience in a non-judgemental or emotionally involved way. Such texts transcribed *verbatim* (word by word) are then scrupulously coded along the four lines that characterize initial coding.

This section synthetically presents procedural indications without slipping into the technicalities so many are filled with because, as stated earlier, closing coding processes up in excessively detailed and rigid technical prescriptions ends up impoverishing the heuristic ability of the researcher. Indeed, his or her theoretical sensitivity remains the most refined tool of analysis. What is more, rigid procedures of analysis risk generating predetermined outcomes.

- First of all, it is necessary to listen to the recordings several times before transcribing and then to *read and re-read* all the texts, especially interviews. Without several overall readings of the text, GT users risk overlooking the linguistic and environmental context in which the words that will then be thoroughly dissected were generated. This procedure, borrowed here from the phenomenological tradition, serves to prepare the researcher to listen to the phenomenon and grasp the overall meaning of a text through a comprehensive reading (Giorgi, 1985; Giorgi & Giorgi, 2003).
- A second step is *word by word* coding. Glaser argues that his attention to the meticulous reading of a text (*explicitation de texte*) in order to allow precisely what the author meant to say emerge, derived from his literature studies in France, at the Sorbonne (Glaser, 1998, p. 24). Scholars wishing to respect the value of the word, its ability to generate meanings, must work very close to the text to allow the author's precise intended meaning to emerge or rise to the surface without

adding arbitrary interpretations (or controlling them). It is not always necessary to conduct coding with such a high level of sophistication. Undoubtedly, however, textual reading or literary textual analysis skills will help researchers to identify a number of codes that might shed light on the meaning of the text, including beyond the denotative level. The focus can then shift to the use of the language to analyse its style, structure, syntactic structures, lexical choices and the use of figures of speech and in particular metaphors, devices which are particularly revealing of much wider discourses.

- Through *line by line* coding, the minimal segments of text which are meaningful for the research question can be selected. These meaning units can be constituted by whole paragraphs, phrases or sentences. It is important to highlight where the segment of text considered for coding begins and ends, and it may overlap with other ones. Also, silences or omissions must be subject to line by line coding as well because they represent indexical expressions that evoke meanings worth interpreting and scrutinizing. The following step is to constantly compare the various codes that have emerged with each other so that further theoretical suggestions might emerge, directions that the researcher will return to in the following coding phases.

To increase the credibility of the analytical structure's anchoring in the data, however, it can be useful for several independent coders to compare among the same text. In this case, inter-coder agreement cannot be measured by any index. But discursive negotiation among the meanings different coders have attributed to the same text provides a further element of comparison, alongside a comparison of the different perspectives that led each coder to highlight the same text differently.

Classic GT also mentions *incident-by-incident* comparison. This suggests comparing not only textual elements but also episodes captured especially during observation and, hence, recorded in field notes or early descriptive memos. These might become evident, in particular, when subjects' behaviours in context are observed from the outside (such as, for instance, an observer watching children in a classroom during a math lesson), without the chance to interact. In this case, I prefer to suggest coding tools which are closely linked to the data and recorded in them in detail. The point of comparing both similar and dissimilar episodes recorded in the data with each other is to trigger ideas and insights. Allowing what is not immediately

Table 5 Example: Interview with a Middle School Literature Teacher on Practices for Integrating Foreign Students

Transcription	**Codes**	***Notes***
R: In general, in your classroom or in the school, are there activities of intercultural education or of the promotion of cultures?		
I: Yes … yes, there are. Because sometimes among us teachers we talk about it even more than once and when we do the planning, well, we do go into details in the subjects, but we also underline this aspect and there is also a sensitivity on the part of the teachers. And when we talk about it among ourselves, we are surprised if small episodes happen, I have mentioned one, similar to these. We are surprised that they happen and we tell ourselves that we should intervene, how to intervene and we talk about it in individual classes. By doing a bit of civic education, when there is the opportunity, or through specific pieces from reading anthologies, the literature teacher mostly makes the students do this activity. But also other teachers, I don't know, other subjects, foreign languages for instance, are able to, or try to, they say that they try to ensure that these kids are integrated, that's it. In one way or another, and even with this form of appreciation and that one can also understand the culture of the other, that it is not only the other who has to learn. How? This is the difficulty. Concretely, I would think like that, but I don't know how to do in a way to make it appreciated. I made some attempts and I would say that it has been more a bluff than anything else.	Interculture against curricular planning Wonder, surprise Interculture within civic education Interculture within anthological readings Literature teacher primacy Proceeding by trial and error Interculture as a tool for integration. 'How? This is the difficulty' Interculture as pretence ('bluff') 'it has been more a bluff than anything else'	*Uncertainty. Evasive, thoughtful, not enthusiastic answer.* *In fact, he didn't answer the question: there is no interculture, if anything, civic education, episodic, sporadic, autonomous, neither planned nor interdisciplinary* *In vivo. Difficulty of putting into practice an idea perception of didactic failure.* *In vivo*

Transcription	**Codes**	***Notes***
R: Why do you say that?		
I: Well, for instance, not this year, but in the previous years, I tried to talk about Islam. Islam is in the history curriculum, these kids who are part of the religion should know it better. Or because they know their religion less, well maybe if we ask one of ours to speak, to illustrate the Catholic religion they don't know how to illustrate it, just to say, or it is equally for that reason. I would have ensured that, instead, to make the lesson more active, that this kid or these kids talked more, about theirs. To valorise it or so. I said that it was a bluff, because instead of valorising they didn't know ... it depended on the fact that maybe they were like that ... not aware, they were not able to convey.	Teaching Islam Involving foreign kids Interculture and history Failure of direct involvement	 *'ours' identifies belonging to the group*
I tried, I would have tried to ensure it was valorised … to not … that is … better than making one of them talk about this topic, there wasn't instead … he didn't manage. Other small things etc. The difficulty, basically, is this: valorising is thought of, but how? Generally, the problem is there, and it is felt, there is sensitivity: we don't know what to do concretely. I initially said that we wanted to hear, for instance this meeting with Xxx, to see what the teachers can do, which was useful yes, but afterwards in practice one doesn't know how to translate it, what to do. Also because, let's say, afterward the practical and concrete activities that we have are to handle a classroom, in which there is also, a … I don't know a non-European, but it's not like one can do it just to …	Praising culture of origin Difficulty putting into practice activities as a response to a perceived problem sensitivity to the problem Practical inefficiency of the update Doubts, uncertainties Theory versus practice Expectations about training Defining uncertainty Non-European	

visible or understandable from a descriptive viewpoint to emerge requires the ability to grasp apparently insignificant details and produce new insights and understandings by connecting them with others. This is the kind of investigative ability possessed by great detectives or the curiosity, elevated to method, that many of us have when entering an unknown house for the first time and forming a mental image of the owners by observing their paintings, smells, books (or lack thereof), furniture choices, degree of cleanliness, decorations, pictures and so on.

5.1.2 *Organization of Coding and Use of Software*

To prepare for the initial coding, for instance of an interview transcription, it is useful to print the text out leaving a wide margin (at least 6 cm) on the right side of the paper. The conceptual labels that codes for each unit can then be put to one side of the selected text. Some people use different coloured highlighters and others not only code but also add notes and comments about the process on the margin of the page.

Such a paper and pencil approach has the advantage of extreme flexibility, and the concreteness of paper enables material closeness with the text. However, a problem arises when all the codes added to date must be listed or when it is time to connect some of them with others that might have already emerged at another stage. In light of these issues, researchers have traditionally been advised (Lincoln & Guba, 1985) to rewrite (or photocopy) the parts of highlighted text and to code them onto index cards and place these in alphabetical order in a card index so that they can be subsequently identified outside of their connection to the text as well.

The advent of computers has offered efficient solutions to old problems of filing and interrogating the data in an orderly manner, but it has created new ones. Labels can be added to the text with a common word processing programme and located in an orderly way on another file, perhaps organized thematically by categories, thanks to a simple copy-paste operation. Otherwise, 'comments' tools can be used to assign a label to a

Table 6 Example of Coding Table

	codes	**notes**
1		
2		
3		

highlighted portion of text. However, this system likewise ultimately offers only a single key for interrogating the data and relocates the quotes outside their native context. Personally, I find it more convenient to gather all the created codes into a table with numbered rows that also includes a cell for possible notes or references to other codes.

A spreadsheet programme can then be used to design a table that works as a database for importing whole texts, codes and pieces of text and synthetically organizing references among them.

To simultaneously conduct the coding work on the texts (albeit by reducing the number of underscores and non-essential notes that remain on the text permanently) and manage a database for archiving codes and subsequent categories, a software for qualitative data analysis called Computer Assisted Qualitative Data Analysis (CAQDAS) was developed in the 1990s. Many of these programmes were designed principally to allow analyses uses GT, such as ATLAS.ti, which was developed using Strauss and Corbin's (1990) approach as a model for what to implement, or more recently MAXQDA (Gibbs, 2018). The forefather of the current NVivo, Nudist (Non-numerical, Unstructured Data Indexing, Searching and Theory-building), was also developed by a computer engineer together with a qualitative health researcher and based on GT. Indeed, unlike other qualitative method analysis, GT provided a clear logic for theory building and procedures to implement flux diagrams and algorithms (Morse & Richards, 2002).

Although such software packages do not represent a real methodological revolution, they do combine the functions of a sophisticated word processor, an essential database capable of archiving and managing texts, and a text retrieval software all at once. The most widespread software in the world today is NVivo (having reached version 12.2 at the time of writing), developed by the Australian company QSR International. To summarize its tools in brief and only as regards the needs of a grounded theorist needs, NVivo allows users to:

- import text and intervene on it while leaving the original text unaltered;
- file in an orderly manner by separating the various types of data, codes and memos;
- write and connect up memos;
- create relationships among documents, codes and memos; to manage images and videos;
- do open and focused coding and then manage the categories by organizing them into a tree structure which remains editable;

- interrogate the text and codes with Boolean indicators (which allow users to refine the research by using key words through the interposition of signs such as 'and', 'not' or 'or' among the search words);
- create and manage diagrams with reference to the texts and categories;
- create effective presentations with good-looking outcomes of results such as word-clouds, maps, diagrams and so on.

In sum, software undeniably helps with the rational storage of documents and analyses (especially when, as is often the case, there is a large among of data to handle), the organization of the working space, and making the process of analysis transparent (the step that makes external audits possible). At the same time, however, these packages can be somehow risky; many scholars thus advise against using them, as they could alter the research experience. In fact, users need to master the method very well if they hope to use software without the software's own possible functions taking over. It is important to be particularly cautious when using precisely those functions that seem most useful, therefore, because they make certain key stages mechanical. One example would be the queries that are possible and effective only on the condition that the conceptual labels and categories have been entered in a uniform and, possibly, standardized manner so that they can be retrieved. Such a condition clashes with an open approach to coding, however, an approach that is more interpretative and closely tied to the text.

5.1.3 *Naming Processes*

Once the meaningful portions of text that say something about the investigated phenomenon have been identified, the question is how to name them. This stage of conceptualization is rather arduous and, although still largely descriptive and firmly grounded in the data, it requires particular theoretical sensitivity to successfully summarize the multiple meanings of a sentence or an episode in a linguistic expression. Indeed, denomination in initial coding is not definitive; the names are only labels which have been temporarily attributed to the codes which recapitulate portions of text; these will not necessarily be developed into categories. Capturing a concept in a synthetic verbal expression is not simple, and the task depends almost entirely on the language used in coding (Tarozzi, 2019). For example, some languages, such as Italian and other neo-Latin languages, are more descriptive and better able to describe meaningful segments of text with long and accurate codes. They are thus particularly suitable in early stages of coding. Others, such as English or Chinese, have strong synthetizing and conceptualizing power and are therefore better for sorting and conceptualizing in the more advanced stages.

I have argued elsewhere (Tarozzi, 2011) that coders in GT are not obliged to choose one language over another. The advantage of pluri-linguistic coding is that working through more languages is not only possible but, to some extent, even beneficial when this allows the researcher to label concepts in a more sophisticated way and then capture phenomena in the analysis.

In GT research practice, first Glaser (1978) and then Charmaz (2006) have suggested using '-ing forms' to express codes. According to Charmaz, a gerund 'fosters theoretical sensitivity because these words nudge us out of static topics and into enacted processes' (Charmaz, 2006, p. 136). Labels can be formed by a verb (in its -ing form) that dynamically expresses their movement, the trajectory of meaning that the coder wants to highlight, perhaps complemented by a noun that precisely identifies the object, content or meaning to which the text refers. Using gerunds is not the only possible way to name the labels given to the first codes, but it can certainly help in making the designations evocative, dense and eloquent but at the same time well rooted in the data. Unfortunately, this verbal form with this particular function does not exist in many neo-Latin languages. This is not necessarily a problem for non-native English speakers like myself; however, very often, while working in Italian, it occurs to me to code in English, using-ing forms, exactly because of English's flexibility in synthetically expressing dense concepts and to better emphasize action and processes.

One of the risks of this phase is resorting to a technical dictionary when coding, drawn from the academic literature on the topic, or, in other words, using non-sensitizing concepts. It is normal for researchers to master the scientific area that they are investigating and, hence, they are inclined to use area language through the expressions, coded in literature, that express what they are observing most effectively and rigorously. In this phase, however, it is actually preferable not to use such expressions. They should be avoided because they tend to enclose the richness of the meanings evoked by the participants inside rigid, closed definitions that attract many and diverse meanings and, necessarily, reduce such meanings into shared, objective formalizations. Suffice to recall terms, found in various disciplines, such as 'resilience', 'metacognition', 'consumer behaviour', 'social capital', or 'bullying'. Just to be clear, at this stage it is not a matter of mature categories that can, and in fact will, need to engage with the literature on the theme, but of initial codes. Such codes essentially serve as handles for picking up significant text excerpts and carrying them during the coding process. Let us not forget that, in the advanced phases of the analysis, researchers are working mainly with the codes and so they will need to be pertinent to the original text and semantically self-sufficient, in the sense that they will need to be meaningful in themselves even without including the text to which they refer. The goal is to maintain this pertinence to the text and avoid distorting it by meaning something else, instead maintaining the evocative power of the raw data. To do so it is important to avoid enclosing the text in all-encompassing jargon, which would inevitably impoverish the expressive liveliness of the words used by participants. In a certain way, some technical incompetence is a virtue in the initial coding, in the sense that it allows suggestive and effective expressions and codes to emerge. These codes are expressed in the form of sensitizing concepts, conceptual labels which are sensitizing precisely by virtue of being naive and not prejudiced by lengthy, consolidated academic experience in that area. Since it would be implausible to hope (or theorize) that good research can be carried out only by unskilled and unexperienced people, however, a typical procedure of GT is *in vivo* coding. This could be defined as coding that uses participants' own words to name concepts. It is a strategy that helps to preserve the richness of meaning that the participants assign to their own actions and views and, at the same time, avoids the risk of stiffening and impoverishing data within technical-academic lexicon. In the example provided on p. 108 a particularly evocative statement by the teacher is coded *in vivo* 'it has been more a bluff than anything else'.

5.1.4 Focused Coding

Initial coding ends by highlighting some 'proto-concepts', which in this phase are 'labelled phenomena' (Strauss & Corbin, 1998, p. 103) – categories still in a draft form and not yet saturated that we prefer to call 'codes'. The analytical material at this point consists of at least a hundred codes drawn from open analysis of the texts and some reflections contained in the memos that accompanied the coding. All this allows the researcher to broaden the sample by suggesting new subjects to interview, following theoretical sampling. The initial research question would have been further refined or new permutations would have been added to it, thus requiring new data; this time, the data will be more focused because they are produced by a new collection, more targeted in that it is guided by the concepts that emerged from the first coding. In this phase and especially beginning with the second step, it can be useful to draft a first coding map.

However chaotic and scattered such a map may be, it can serve to identify the connections among conceptualizations and highlight salient concepts as compared to less relevant ones.

During focused coding, the phase of taking off from the runway of description towards the skies of conceptualization begins. This step is not simple. It is difficult for the neophyte researcher to abandon his or her reassuring empirical proximity to the data, even though in the long run such proximity would only lead to systematic and organized descriptions. And yet abandoning it is necessary to surrender to the thrill of theorization, allowing insights from the data to emerge by relying not so much on repeated reading of the data or further collection as on indulging the creative capacity for insight that stems from theoretical sensitivity. Let us not forget that coding, in all of its phases, is a process of surfacing. The act of abandoning the descriptive level for the conceptual one, no matter how difficult and too often excessively prolonged, starts precisely in this phase. This point reminds me of the unique personality of two of my best doctoral students. L. and F. were both extremely brilliant students, both competent in GT method and procedures, but with two different and complementary skill sets and attitudes. One of them, L., was trained in philosophy and theology and had developed a great capacity for conceptualization and abstraction. He was excellent at creating links among very distant concepts, inducting macro categories and broader concepts from them, and providing careful and detailed theoretical definitions. On the other hand, he sometimes ran the risk of forgetting the empirical roots of these concepts, and his beautiful theoretical constructions or theories were sometimes overly speculative rather than grounded. The other, F., was trained as a cultural anthropologist with significant experience in ethnographic field work and participant observation. She was able to write a 10,000-word description from 30 minutes of observation. She was also talented in initial open coding, during which she carefully detected hundreds of codes describing the data. On the other hand, F. sometimes faced difficulties in letting insights emerge and guessing, hypothesizing and postulating abstract categories and her theory building sometimes lacked conceptual and explanatory power. Luckily, they were close friends, capable of cooperating, and although they often bickered around analytical steps, they were also able to complement each other's strengths and weaknesses to form an incredible GT team.

The aim of focused coding is to collect concepts into categories and identify concepts at a higher level of abstraction, but it is also the level on which the categories start connecting to each other and with their properties. It may thus begin already with the first step of collection/analysis and, in fact, in some ways it chronologically overlaps with initial coding. If open coding fragments the data, distinguishing and analytically separated them, this phase begins a synthetic process: searching for lines of coherence among them. This phase can be seen to comprise two main processes.

Identifying macro concepts. Wider concepts; salient themes with the capacity to interpret broader portions of data. These concepts or proto-categories arise more frequently but, above all, with more intensity. They are also significantly dense, conceptually departing from the purely descriptive level. For example, in a GT study on the individual and socio-cultural assumptions underlying teenagers' criminal behaviours, the researchers (Lopez & Emmer, 2000) conducted initial coding that produced around 350 conceptual labels; they then grouped them according to similarity in broader categories (for instance, various types of compensation for criminal acts are grouped in the category *crime rewards*). Therefore, at the end of the initial coding about 40 phenomena emerged and were labelled 'foundations for the choice of the victim', 'perception of the sanctions' or 'internal conflicts between beliefs and behaviours'.

Connecting the categories with each other and these with sub-categories and defining their properties. This phase is about interrogating and comparing the emerged categories with each other. After drawing connections among some concepts, the researcher reflects on the nature of these connections: there are broader categories, parents encompassing sibling-categories. There are also sister-categories with the same level of abstraction. Subsequently, analysts raise questions about their properties – conditions, dimensions and circumstances – and they identify the possible answers that emerge from the comparative comparison, or realize that the category is not yet saturated and therefore requires further data. Both Glaser and Strauss & Corbin proposed several strategies for identifying coding families or properties, and Strauss and Corbin in particular proposed precise guidelines for identifying and classifying properties and relations between categories along several dimension, called Axial coding. This strategy is very rigid, however, and has been one of the most contentious aspects of GT.

Beyond any excessive technicalities, what is important in this phase is to let the conceptual categories emerge and connect them with each other, identifying their characteristics and conditions of existence.

There is a very practical technique, so simple as to appear as trivial, that I have used many times that does a good job of clarifying the meaning of the abductive logic that guides this phase. Specifically, it involves:

- sorting the codes developed through initial coding into groups;
- trying to name these groups;
- creating links among them;
- defining conceptual hierarchies among them (the direction of the links);
- naming the links among them (causal, temporal);
- interrogating categories and their links with questions (e.g. under what conditions do they have meaning for the participants?; what consequences do they have?; how do they arise?; when, where, why; who are the actors?; who is subjected to the actions?)

If you can locate clear answers to these questions in the data, then you have dynamic pictures of some categories for your emerging theory. If not, this means that you need more data. In keeping with the principle of theoretical sampling, however, you now know *what kind of data* you need.

To return to the previous example, the categories in that research were further reduced by identifying connections among the forty categories that had emerged. The phenomenon of delinquent behaviour assumed particular importance and its properties were examined according to different parameters: precrime and contributing conditions, the context that influenced it, the strategies of action and interaction through which it was put into practice and the consequences of these actions or interactions. From this intersection, four emergent salient typologies of criminal action stood out (aggression, theft, crimes related to drugs, group crimes) which were then cross-bred with three types of reasons that had likewise emerged from the data, reasons guiding the delinquent behaviour (emotions-driven, beliefs-driven, reward-driven). A good method for highlighting the relationships among the categories and sub-categories to place them inside a double-entry table so as to identify the elements of comparison, certainly conceptual rather than numerical, and to fill the significant intersections with meaning. For instance, in the research mentioned earlier

Table 7 Comparison of the Processes of Emancipation and Assimilation in the Integration of Some Foreign Students

	Emancipation	**Assimilation**
Expectations on subject learning	*Academic achievement*: respecting learning timeframes	*Selection*: no preferential track
Teaching Italian as L2	Tool of knowledge and empowerment: *social integration*	Tool to Italianize. *Social exclusion*
Teaching in the classroom	Socialization	Lack of individualization
Special projects outside the classroom	Individualization	Distancing the problematic case

Source: Tarozzi (2006).

on the integration practices of non-national students, some concepts emerged that identified more widespread practices; at the same time, there appeared to be some models, mostly implicit, that guided actions. In particular, two salient dynamics emerged, emancipation and assimilation, which granted different connotations to the same educational and didactic practices (Tarozzi, 2006).

5.1.5 Theoretical Coding

The coding processes in the previous phases, just like each subsequent step of data collection/analysis, are guided by an aim that becomes gradually more evident to the point of appearing explicit and clear in this phase: searching for the *core category*. Without this direction, theoretical coding ends up dispersed along various meandering paths, lacking a unitary sense. A *core category* is a key concept, the central, nuclear or essential category that organizes the set of categories. Also defined as *central category* (Strauss & Corbin, 1998, p. 146) or *core variable* (Glaser, 1998), it represents the basic social process that sums up a behavioural or social concept actors use to act in a certain context with reference to a certain theme. This concept is tentacular; it unifies the categories and accounts for variations in the data. It is a concept that expresses intense analytical power. It is saturated, dense but porous, and capable of integrating the categories by virtue of being highly branched within them. It is complete and has great explanatory power. Around it – developed in terms of its properties and relationships, and analytically formulated – we can build the model that defines the theory we were looking for. This is the heart of the final theorization of a

GT research project, and in fact this concept is often used as the title of the research report that ends up being written. The central categories are often expressed in a very evocative, weighty form, by carefully choosing words that are dense in meaning: 'awareness of dying' (Glaser & Strauss, 1965), 'vagueing out' (Rizzo, 1993), 'enduring and expression of suffering' (Amankwaa, 2005; Morse & Carter, 1996) or 'super-normalization processes' (Charmaz, 1973, 1987), that is, the attitude of chronic patients when they flaunt a normality in their actions that is actually prevented by their disease.

Finding and focusing on the *core category(ies)* is the aim of theoretical coding, the coding phase that takes place at the highest level of conceptual abstraction. In this phase the researcher, having identified the categories, their properties and initial relationships, proceeds through insights to leap forward and return to the data; he or she gives shape to the theory, both by identifying analytical hierarchies among the categories and by proposing insights, conjectures or advanced inferences the data-rootedness of which will then need to be verified. The two main schools have denominated this phase differently, the distinction between *selective coding* (Strauss & Corbin, 1998) and *theoretical coding* (Glaser, 1978, 1998) is more than lexical. The distinction significantly changes the aim of this phase and its expected theoretical outcome just as it changes the analytical procedures used to achieve results: for Glaser these procedures are more theoretical and intuitive, while for Strauss & Corbin they are more descriptive and analytical. Readers are advised to consult those texts for an accurate understanding of the coding schemes those schools propose, schemes which are useful especially for training and developing one's own theoretical sensitivity rather than adopting a standardized technique. In this section I provide suggestions for managing the theoretical building task by highlighting the objectives rather than the techniques, the perspectives rather than the recipes, the conceptual steps rather than the kind of technical jargon which provides a shared name and outwardly legitimizes procedures and results.

Four conceptual steps of this phase can be summarized, as mentioned in Chapter 3:

- developing the categories;
- connecting the categories with each other;
- identifying the core category;
- integrating and defining the theory.

Developing the categories. Focused coding produces categories that require polishing. These are methodically defined through theoretical coding, in which further data collection thins out in favour of analytical thinking about the codes, memos and categories identified, always considered in the data in which they are rooted. For instance, a research study intending to explore the actions that parents enact to protect one child when another sibling suffers from anorexia shed light on the five main categories: maintaining normality, compensating for changes in routine, protecting siblings, providing emotional support, and managing the consequences (Honey & Halse, 2007).

Connecting the categories (relationships and hierarchy). Categories always emerge in relationship with each other. Analysing the relationships among the categories means carrying out three distinct operations:

1. connecting the categories with each other and conceptualizing the type of relationship that joins them;
2. developing (deductively and not inductively) the categories with sub-categories on the basis of each of their properties and size;
3. placing the categories in hierarchical relationship by identifying macro categories that include smaller categories. Categories are not all equal; they are differentiated by frequency (number of empirical occurrences found for each one), conceptual scale, density and so on. A good system of theoretical coding is therefore to define hierarchical relationships among each other that identify sister categories and daughter categories: those in a relationship of hierarchical equality, and those that are sub-categories which can be placed under the umbrella of a more conceptually extended category. For instance, let us look at the hierarchical relationships identified among the categories developed as part of a research study on the initial factors that lead freshmen to prematurely abandon their university degree (Rausch & Hamilton, 2006)

Identifying the core category. The *core category* is the main organizing concept of a research area that can be identified inductively, by hierarchically arranging the categories that have emerged from the data. The task of identifying it is helped by not only creating diagrams and visualizations (see section 6.2) but also writing long memos (see section 6.1), especially if expressed in a *narrative* way. In fact, this underlying process assumes definition in the story that connects up analytical elements which are

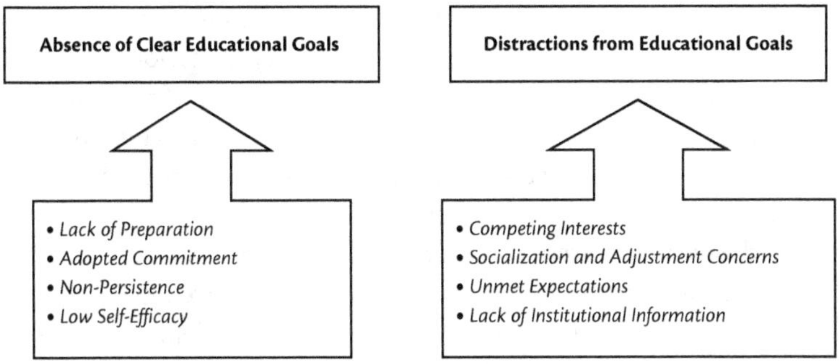

Figure 7 Selective categories representing GT (from Rausch and Hamilton, 2006, p. 330).

distant and detached from each other. It identifies the pathway (or, one possible pathway) that makes sense of the whole.

The core category will never appear as a mechanical consequence of meticulous analytical work. Rather, it is the result of an insight, something which is by definition sudden and unexpected. However, the careful analytical work of abstraction and synthesis creates the conditions for it to emerge.

Theoretical coding aims to provide an integrated interpretation with the power to unite the various analytical text passages induced from the data through the various levels of coding into a single picture. It recounts a coherent analytical story that not only specifies the categories which emerged and clarifies the horizontal and vertical relationships that connect them but also and especially achieves a unified vision which in turn drives the conceptualization towards ever-higher levels of abstraction. From within this story identifying the hierarchies and relationships among the concepts rises the progressive construction of a theory. By characterizing, developing and refining concepts and relationships, the theory is built discursively.

Integrating and defining the theory. Identifying, or constructing, the *core category* per se is not the arrival point of GT. The *core category* answers the research question, now finally expressed in its definitive form, and the process of identifying this category has essentially two aims:

1. *Delimiting the theory.* During the course of coding many categories emerge, and the analysis could be sent in a number of different

directions by powerful and dispersive centrifugal forces. Researchers must thus know how to define the theory, consciously excluding some categories and themes from the light cone of analytical focus which, although relevant, would not be manageable to pursue. Identifying the core category marks the route towards delimiting the scope of the research in a way that is neither arbitrary nor dictated exclusively by external reasons (depletion of resources, deadlines, tiredness, pressure from the supervisor). Moreover, it is only at this point that the research question assumes its definitive form: the selective coding that leads to the core *variable*, Glaser writes, 'means that the analyst delimits his coding to only those variables that relate to the core variable in sufficiently significant ways to be used in a parsimonious theory' (Glaser, 1978, p. 61). The conceptual space thus defined by the core category is the site in which theoretical elaboration takes place, usually expressed as a model or conceptual map illustrating the process the researcher set out to analyse.

2. *To open up the researcher to new questions and new comparisons* in order to characterize and explore the basic general process. Here the researcher conceptualizes the questions by selectively returning to the data and then integrating everything into a unitary interpretative model. The categories are developed in the light of some coding devices formulated differently from the various schools: Glaser proposes conceptualizing the main categories by interrogating them with the '6 Cs' (causes, contexts, contingencies, consequences, co-variations and conditions) (Glaser, 1978, further specified and enhanced in 1998), while Strauss and Corbin suggest reading them in the light of properties, sizes and range of variation (Strauss & Corbin, 1998).

The set of categories, fully developed in terms of their properties and the relationships among them, is not yet the theory a GT user is looking to build. It is necessary at this point to integrate the categories and themes that have emerged into a (single) model that explains the theoretical process connecting them.

This conceptual operation, different in nature from the previous ones (now synthetic instead of analytical) requires identifying the basic social process and its links with the context in which it emerged. Subsequently, the main knots of the basic process will have to be gradually developed

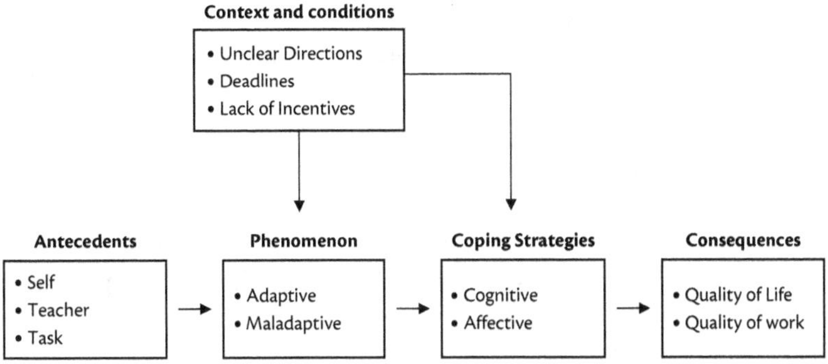

Figure 8 Explanatory model of the processes of academic procrastination.
Source: Schraw, Wadkins and Olafson (2007)

and expanded until they constitute the various focused strands of the investigation, converging and strengthening the general theory. This is what happened with the general model presented in Chapter 3 in relation to the process of TV family governance (cfr. p.).

Another example of a general model comes from a study on academic procrastination (Schraw, Wadkins, & Olafson, 2007) that produced the following paradigmatic model (outlined in Figure 8), a model that constitutes the backbone of this GT in relation to procrastination processes.

5.2 Theoretical Sampling

One of GT's main original contributions is the introduction of a sampling strategy for qualitative inquiry which represents an equally rigorous and theoretically well-founded alternative to probabilistic sampling on a statistical basis. It is a way of selecting participants and units of analysis which are closely connected and functional to the process of coding and analysis. Glaser defines it as 'the process of data collection for generating theory whereby the analyst jointly collects, codes, and analyses his data and decides what data to collect next and where to find them, in order to develop his theory as it emerges' (Glaser, 1978, p. 36).

This type of sampling requires the researcher to collect data and engage in analysis simultaneously. The very logic of theoretical sampling is structurally different from the forms of random, statistically based sampling designed to identify the number of subjects necessary and sufficient to guarantee the representativeness of the sample in relation to the overall universe of the subjects, so as to guarantee the generalizability of the results (Morse & Clark, 2019). However, it is equally distinct from purely subjective forms of case selection dictated by convenience or accessibility that reject the very concept of sample because some qualitative research methods are essentially descriptive or idiographic, that is, they refer to particular cases and are thus not generalizable.

In GT, the role of sampling is intimately linked to theory building. It is what enables the process of conceptual formulation and guides the analytical process of devising and refining the categories and properties that constitute the theory.

How does theoretical sampling work in the initial steps of the process? The first step consists of choosing some cases according to the logic of *purposive* sampling, that is, by looking for a series of cases, already quite differentiated among themselves, in contexts in which the phenomena under investigation are likely to manifest in a significant manner. This step is the only theoretical sampling step that can be planned in advance and so the only one for which a researcher can predict timing, costs and modes of accessing the field and take into consideration the ethical implications. The definitive size of the sample, instead, will not be defined until the research is concluded and the theory fully elaborated. This is why this essential and unavoidable feature of GT is also one of the steps users most often neglect. In fact, researchers quite often define the sample on which to conduct their analysis in advance or reduce GT to its analytical aspects, detached from sample formation and data collection.

Later, theoretical sampling suggests ways of answering the question: where can I find further cases to use for the comparison following the first collection? (Glaser & Strauss, 1967). For instance, to investigate the emotional and cognitive factors that lead to suicide attempts in teenagers, the researcher will have to obtain access to the cases of teens who had this experience and agree to talk about it. He or she might contact social and health services or post adverts in newspapers and on notice boards or particular websites to make contact with an initial group of subjects (Everall, Bostik, & Paulson, 2006). The following cases will be selected on the basis of the suggestions flowing from the theory. In particular, the researcher will look for the relevant cases that answer the unanswered questions found in the memos accompanying the various phases of analysis, always with the intent of fostering constant comparison. The study would thus proceed by looking for similarities and differences within the cases and groups taken into consideration: the task is to identify similar phenomena appearing in different contexts or dissimilar phenomena in the same contexts, like investigating the experience of dying in different types of hospital departments (intensive care, emergency department, oncology, etc.) or differentiating according to artificially constructed classes such as age, gender, social class, ethnicity and so on by always maximizing and minimizing both the differences and the similarities or by deliberately pursuing negative cases that disprove the emerging theory. Ultimately, however, the process of widening the sample clearly requires having formulated or at least drafted some categories, otherwise there is no theoretical sampling.

An emblematic example of theoretical sampling is drawn from a memo produced as part of Glaser and Strauss' research on the awareness of dying (Glaser & Strauss, 1965). Indeed, this memo highlights with great clarity the progress of theoretical sampling in that research study (Glaser & Strauss, 1967, p. 59):

> Visits to the various medical services were scheduled as follows: I wished first to look at services that minimized patient awareness (and so first looked at a premature baby service and then at a neurosurgical service where patients were frequently comatose). I wished next to look at dying in a situation where expectancy of staff and often of patients was great and dying was quick, so I observed on an Intensive Care Unit. Then I wished to observe on a service where staff expectations of terminality were great but where the patient's might or might not be, and where dying tended to be slow. So I looked next at a cancer service. I wished then to look at conditions where death was unexpected and rapid, and so looked at an emergency service. While we were looking at some different types of services, we also observed the above types of service at other types of hospitals. So our scheduling of types of service was directed by a general conceptual scheme – which included hypotheses about awareness, expectedness and rate of dying – as well as by a developing conceptual structure including matters not at first envisioned. Sometimes we returned to services after the initial two or three or four weeks of continuous observation, in order to check upon items which needed checking or had been missed in the initial period.

Figure 3 (p. 47) clearly shows that, unlike other types of sampling which are developed only in the first phases of research, theoretical sampling is a recurrent activity in the GT process. It accompanies and guides various phases of the data collection and analysis, at different levels of theorization. At first, it is applied to extant data to select further units of analysis from which to collect new data. Subsequently, it is applied to the categories and their properties to accompany the more conceptually advanced coding phases. In both cases, it results in further collection of data, expanding the data collection into new areas and new participants.

Once the different logic underlying theoretical sampling is understood, it becomes clear that this technique goes beyond a simple instrument for defining quantity and characteristics of the research participants (although it also does this). Indeed, it becomes a powerful and versatile tool for data analysis. By minimizing and maximizing differences in comparing groups, theoretical sampling contributes to enhancing the conceptual scope of the emerging theory by guiding the researcher towards even more relevant groups. Respectively, it helps to:

- consolidate, support and strengthen the categories that are perceived as interesting and highly evocative;
- outline the properties of a category;
- identify connections among the categories and between these categories and the properties;
- fill in the gaps of the theory, perceive their possible variations.

When can the data collection be considered complete, however? And a category sufficiently supported by evidence? To answer these questions, the nuanced, complex, equivocal and at times misused concept of 'saturation' comes to our aid.

5.2.1 *Saturation*

The criterion for establishing when to stop sampling cases referring to each category is theoretical saturation. It has been argued that a category is saturated when new data provide neither new properties for a category nor further insights about the theory (Bryant & Charmaz, 2007). Saturation is achieved by proceeding with the theoretical development of the categories. When the data become redundant in the sense that any new data collected serve only to confirm the categories and their properties, this means that new data are no longer necessary for developing a category. Of course, to obtain saturation it is necessary to honestly follow the directions suggested by theoretical sampling: specifically, to allow negative or deviant cases to emerge, to reveal situations which, by being inconsistent with the categories drafted up to that point, can highlight the theory's lacunae and weaknesses, the points in which it cannot be said to be properly empirically grounded. There is no doubt that negative cases only help theoretical sampling if they emerge from the analysis. If they are imported from the outside, instead, they represent a different form of sample validation that may be used in other methods but has nothing to do with GT (Charmaz, 2006).

How to establish with the necessary accuracy and reliability required that a given category is saturated and any further collection useless would be difficult and controversial (Morse, 1995, 2015). Glaser and Strauss dismiss this matter by stating that 'the criteria for determining saturation ... are a combination of the empirical limits of the data, the integration and density of the theory, and the analyst's theoretical sensitivity' (1967, p. 62).

An ambitious study that produces an innovative theory requires the saturation of the categories to be justified rather than merely claimed, just like an investigation that is based on only a few interviews raises legitimate doubts about the effective saturation of its categories and, hence, invalidates the credibility of the theory built around them. For Strauss and Corbin (1998, p. 212), a category is theoretically saturated when:

- no new data referring to a given category emerge;
- the category is well developed in terms of its properties, size and possible variations;
- the relationships among the categories are well established and validated.

Ultimately, it is not enough to claim that the categories and sample are saturated; the research must make explicit *how* such saturation has been obtained (Morse, 1995).

To Sum Up

- In GT, the analysis of data proceeds according to increasing levels of theoretical abstraction. This process is systematic even though it inevitably retains the characteristics of artisanal, procedural knowledge building.
- The analysis progresses along gradual steps of data collection and coding, with precise analytical procedures applied to each of these steps: the *initial coding* remains closely linked to the data; it reads and

breaks down the text in all the directions that this text allows with the aim of identifying some initial conceptual labels. With due caution, this procedure can also be carried out with the aid of specific software. It is followed by *focused coding* aimed at transforming the first concepts into draft categories and at drawing the first connections among them. It is in *theoretical coding* that the categories begin to be most fully defined, and the theorization proceeds in the direction of identifying the core category, the key concept around which the theory will be organized.

- After having developed the categories and placed them in a hierarchical relationship, and identified the *core category*, the theory should be integrated and thematically systematized around the conceptual axes that have emerged from the data.
- Theoretical sampling is the analytical tool, typical of GT, that allows the researcher to choose the cases until they are completely theoretically saturated, a status which must be explicitly justified.

Further Readings

On Coding Strategy

Charmaz, K. (2014). *Constructing Grounded Theory: A Practical Guide through Qualitative Analysis*, 2nd ed. London: Sage.

Corbin, J., & Strauss, A. (2015). *Basics of Qualitative Research: Techniques and Procedures for Developing Grounded Theory*, 4th ed. Thousand Oaks, CA: Sage.

Glaser, B. (1998). *Doing Grounded Theory: Issues and Discussions*. Mill Valley, CA: Sociology Press.

Kelle, U. (2007). The Development of Categories: Different Approaches in Grounded Theory. In A. Bryant, & K. Charmaz (Eds.), *The SAGE Handbook of Grounded Theory*. Los Angeles: Sage, 191–213.

Thornberg, R., & Charmaz, K. (2014). Grounded Theory and Theoretical Coding. In U. Flick (Ed.), *The SAGE Handbook of Qualitative Data Analysis*. London: Sage, pp. 153–69.

On Theoretical Sampling

Bryant, A. (2017). *Grounded Theory and Grounded Theorizing: Pragmatism in Research Practice*. New York: Oxford University Press, chap. 12.

Glaser, B. G., & Strauss, A. L. (1967). *The Discovery of Grounded Theory: Strategies for Qualitative Research*. Chicago: Aldine de Gruyter, chap III.

Morse, J. (2007). Sampling in Grounded Theory. In A. Bryant, & K. Charmaz. *The SAGE Handbook of Grounded Theory*. Los Angeles: SAGE, 229–44.

Morse, J., & Clark, L. (2019). The Nuances of Grounded Theory Sampling and the Pivotal Role of Theoretical Sampling. In A. Bryant, & K. Charmaz (Eds.), *The SAGE Handbook of Current Developments in Grounded Theory*. Los Angeles: Sage, 145–66.

On the Use of CAQDA Software

Bazeley, P., & Jackson, K. (2019). *Qualitative Data Analysis with NVivo*, 3rd edn. Los Angeles: Sage.

Gibbs, G. (2018). *Analysing Qualitative Data: The Sage Qualitative Research Kit*, 2nd edn. London: Sage.

Morse, J., & Richards, L. (2002). *Readme First: For a User's Guide to Qualitative Methods*. Thousand Oaks, CA: Sage.

Woolf, N. H., & Silver, C. (2017). *Qualitative Analysis Using ATLAS.ti, NVivo and MAXQDA: The Five-level QDA Method*. London: Routledge.

6 Analysis: The Interpretive Work of Writing

6.1 Memos

> The *core stage* in the process of generating theory, the bedrock of theory generation, its true product is the writing of theoretical memos. If the analyst skips this stage by going directly from coding to sorting or to writing – he *is not* doing grounded theory. (Glaser, 1978, p. 83, italics in the original)

Memos are meta-cognitive devices and spaces for the self-reflective accounts that accompany, support and guide the emergence of the theory in all its phases, from data collection to theoretical coding. In these accounts, researchers record the ideas, insights and conjectures that strike them during data collection and analysis.

Memos perform different functions. First, they are useful for recording the methodological choices made at each point in the process. It is in the memos that GT practitioners organize their theoretical sampling, decide when a category is saturated and, if not, where to go looking for the further data required and redefine the research question. While a product is generated through the various phases of coding, it is the memos that keep track of the *process* that led to that product. Memos not only provide the basis for the final write-up but also demonstrate the credibility of the work, seeing as, in qualitative research, reliability stems from the opportunity to provide an account of the way in which certain results were obtained rather than adherence to external parameters. Secondly, memos are the space for theoretically reflecting on the analytical trajectory; the path that begins from the descriptive level of the data to climb to the theoretical level and 'the original description is subsumed by analysis' (Glaser, 1978, p. 84). The very act of writing memos invites researchers to delve into the implicit side of their own assumptions, to unpack and refine the thoughts that initially manifest as condensed and elusive, to make visible notions that are taken for granted and to unravel the meanings tangled around a concept. Thirdly, memos serve to make pre-existing assumptions, pre-understandings, prejudices and anticipated knowledge explicit. Earlier, I talked about the need to detach from these and to suspend judgement on these assumptions. Memos provide the concrete tools for taking that step back and the space in which the *epoché* (the suspension of judgement or bracketing) takes place. In doing so, the repository of memos also works as a self-reflexive research log. According to my phenomenological perspective, it can be regarded as a tool that allows the observer to make his or her involvement within the observed setting explicit. Researchers are part of the context that they intend to analyse, and they contribute to constructing it; their assumptions, background, visions and knowledge are inevitably part of their view of the phenomena that they want to investigate. This reflexive sensitivity is not a way of chasing some illusory objectivity or eliminating subjective elements, the *bias*, that would pollute the setting, however. Rather, the goal is to not take subjective elements for granted, making them explicit so as to epistemically step back from them. That is how a self-reflective daily research log can contribute to this task.

With the exception of this third function, memos do have essentially an analytical or even meta-empirical scope as the place where the analyst records thoughtful ponderations and sudden insights.

Although memos accompany all the phases of the research, their decisive moment comes in the higher and more abstract phases of coding. Early memos, in initial coding, are generally shorter and more descriptive. They are useful for explaining the directions that open up as the analysis proceeds. For instance, for doctoral students it can be advisable to write long memos to focus their generative research question after a first exploration in the field, immediately before drafting a detailed project. The most advanced memos are essential in GT in that they chart the path that has led to identifying a certain category – how this category has evolved and how it has been redefined. Above all, however, they are the place for constant comparison. It is here that the reflections comparing various subjects, conceptual labels, categories and the properties of the categories and so on, take shape.

The are no fixed rules for writing memos. In fact, it is vital that all analysts develop their own style because carving out these spaces of freedom is essential for stimulating the creativity necessary to allow ideas to emerge. Nevertheless, it is also important for the memos to be orderly and accurate, so that it is easy to locate them later. For this reason, a memo must always contain the date, a title and the documents it is connected to, whether they are written on papers or in files or indicated using CAQDAS software. It is critical to write memos regularly, especially during moments of progress: key moments such as after having identified each category, after each analytical session, after research group meetings or after a meeting with the supervisor. The writing needs to be free so as to allow ideas to emerge, but at the same time, the more refined the memos are the more useful they will be. Therefore, in order to be able to share and use them later, it is advisable to re-read and edit them multiple times and to complete and polish them, adding quotations and complete bibliographic references.

6.2 Narratives and Diagramming

There is one among the various types of memos that constitutes a particularly appropriate tool for accompanying the process of theoretical coding. After having delineated the first categories and identified some relationships of meaning among them, the act of searching for the *core category* and then the problem of integrating the various elements into a single theory capable of explaining the main processes represent a rather acrobatic epistemic jump. In this delicate and complex phase, it helps to narrate a story. Such a storyline retraces the entire course of the research, from the development of the research question through the various turning points and second thoughts up to the formulation of the categories. This narrative serves to identify the *core category* – the phenomenon or incident capable of integrating the analytical narrative. The ideal would be to narrate the story to a good friend who knows nothing about the research, thus obliging the researcher not to take anything for granted when summarizing the steps of the process. Recording your own narration, transcribing and refining it in the form of an advanced memo, undoubtedly represents an excellent strategy.

Such a device is effective because narrating the natural story of a research project (Silverman, 2000), that is, summarizing the steps that led to building a theory, entails identifying the narrative core which is capable of unifying the multiple directions suggested by the categories. Narrating the story of a lengthy research path, like all qualitative paths full of setbacks, corrections, afterthoughts and so on, is an analytical endeavour involving theoretical construction. It requires researchers to interrogate the phenomena and interpretative categories, to identify links and to clearly outline the steps, making many trickling streams converge into a large narrative river with the power to hold everything together meaningfully. The brief story that follows is an example of this type of narrative, one that arose during the analysis and was also reported in the final write-up (Tarozzi, 2007).

> This is the story of how mainly the teachers, but also the principals, give meaning to their intercultural didactic practices in the Trento school. We wanted to identify the good practices that the teachers put in place for welcoming and integrating non-national students into the school. As we proceeded with the data collection and analysis, the idea took shape that practices, before becoming 'good' and being generalized to multiple contexts, need to be described, made meaningful, and placed within theoretical and methodological models capable of explaining, justifying, enlivening, and animating them.
>
> We wanted to explore the processes through which the teachers implemented specific practices when they orient themselves towards welcoming and integrating foreign students, and instead we landed on analysing the meaning (and the name) that they assign to practices that are very different from each other, and the relationships of meaning among them.
>
> The central category, the core category, became: the meaning attributed to interculture by school stakeholders. And, thus, to that umbrella term that includes many different, and often oppositional, meanings. The research aims to clarify what the teachers mean by interculture, to unveil the dynamics of attribution of meaning to the idea of interculture and what practices they locate under this denomination. In fact, we noticed that the different meanings attributed to this notion necessarily give rise to diverse practices and we tried to systematically present the implicit models that organise such practices and to shed light on the operational directions that can be drawn from this analysis.

An analogous process, more familiar to those with a more visual cognitive style, can be carried out by drawing diagrams, conceptual maps or graphs. These visuals allow researchers to overcome the formalization of the categories, to gaze on them from above and, from that detached standpoint, to reflect and synthetically understand the relationships among the concepts. At the start, the diagrams are very simple figures indicating concepts with arrows connecting them, which are useful for uncovering gaps in the theory or categories that are not yet sufficiently saturated. Then, as the analysis delves more deeply, further elements will fill the paper allowing the analyst to reflect on the nature of the relationship connecting the concepts with each other, whether it is associative, symmetrical or unidirectional. The relationship can then be characterized in various ways (causal, temporal or consecutive). Finally, in the course of theoretical coding, the diagrams function to integrate the theory and portray the conceptual model that the researcher has developed even before it can be fully expressed in verbal language. A diagram (see, for instance, Figure 5 (p. 69) that synthesizes the general model of TV family governance) eloquently summarizes the complexity and density of a theory. It does not lay out the theory in detail, but the very act of building the diagram helps the analyst to develop concepts and identify links. It is important to remember that such a visual is an analytical tool, not the final form in which the results will be presented.

The technique of drawing diagrams is a distinctive trait of the schools derived from Strauss in particular and has become a central element of *situational analysis* (Clarke, 2003, 2005). In this approach, situational maps represent an alternative to the way classic GT emphasizes the basic social process; such maps bring the researcher's prior knowledge together with what he or she has empirically gleaned from the data.

However procedurally effective these narrative and graphic devices may be, they cannot substitute for the process of fully formulating the theory; likewise, using such devices should not carry the researcher too far off-track. As with any tool, the risk is that stories and diagrams become an end in themselves or end up confining the researcher's gaze within the boundaries set by the tool itself.

6.3 Writing Up a GT

The very act of writing is a theorization process. Writing a final report – such as a dissertation, book or academic article – should not be conceptualized as something that happens when all the elements have already been formulated, and it is only a matter of extracting these thoughts from the researcher's mind and translating them into a verbal communicative code. Writing *is* thinking, and the theory is constructed also and especially *in* the process of writing. Especially according to a constructivist approach, therefore, writing is not only a device for expressing content but also the main form through which that content is constructed.

In every research project, the final write-up is a critical moment. It is an emotionally engaging process that brings to the surface all our uncertainties, doubts about our work or ability to write. It is not by chance that scholars tend to procrastinate over it so much.

While such issues plague all experiences of research writing, in GT there are fewer difficulties. In this approach, writing does not begin from scratch. The habit of thinking theoretically and of writing down thoughts, producing arguments, developing meanings and looking for supporting evidence should have accompanied the entire research path, through the act of memo writing.

Indeed, in GT, writing should start precisely from the process of scrutinizing the most highly developed memos, as well as any diagrams, which integrate the theory, that is, provide an overview on the global theory or general model that the research has produced. This is followed by a period of immersion in the library that contributes to thickening the theory, systematically comparing the researcher's empirically emergent categories with the pre-existing research found in the relevant literature. Without this dialogue with the current academic debate, GT risks producing predictable, banal and highly simplified results.

Writing the report – whether a doctoral thesis, article or book – is always a project of communication. Therefore, authors need to choose the themes they intend to communicate while bearing in mind the intended recipients of their communication. The analysis does not explain itself, and not everything that emerged from the research can be conveyed. What is needed is a communicative project involving a selected set of themes and effectively organized writing.

It is impossible to define specific writing rules for presenting the results. However, a GT report should grant particular importance to the part describing the development of the research design, not falling into the common trap of neglecting to outline all the procedural steps of this process and how it became clearer over time. Whenever possible, as for instance in a monograph, authors are advised to write a chapter in form of a 'the research story'. Unfortunately, however, it is becoming more and more difficult to publish the results of a study, even a large-scale one, as a book, and standard 6,000-word journal articles do not provide enough space for a complete methodology section. In GT, in particular, the conclusions are also key, and they must outline how the research results might say something relevant to the practitioners.

In writing reports, researchers need to carefully choose what aspects of the theory they want to communicate and then arrange the themes in a coherent and logical structure. These themes then need to be developed in the framework of a sound line of argumentation explicating and clarifying the theses the author would like to present, the overall argument, the rationale and the empirical evidence supporting them. Unlike other qualitative research traditions, in GT the evidence is not provided by extracts from interviews intended to demonstrate the soundness of certain claims. If and when interview excerpts are quoted, and it is always a good practice to do so, it is only because they have significant emblematic power and are effective in illustrating a concept expressed in the text. They do not serve to confirm every single statement, as these assertions are instead corroborated by their being rooted in the research process.

Ultimately, it is essential that the GT says something. A common risk involved in using this rather complex approach is that of following the procedures too closely and being too attached to the procedural directions – guidelines which may be reassuring because they are so rigorous. Researchers may imagine that such adherence protects them from possible accusations that the research lacks rigour. In reality, however, such an approach ensures that the research, no matter how rigorous, will not have much to say; it will not be relevant or significantly increase knowledge in that area. For instance, discovering that the central category of research on the ways parents of anorexic daughters take care of their other children is 'taking care of other children' does not do much to increase knowledge on this theme, even if the *core category* has been formulated in all of its fundamental processes. It is therefore necessary, especially in the writing phase, to exercise creativity. Of course such creativity must always remain grounded in the data, but without creativity the data themselves are mute (and creativity without the data is lame). Having the courage to risk, to dare and to throw yourself into interpretations is a key characteristic of every grounded theorist. Indeed, as the concluding chapter will show, it deserves a place beside the procedural rigour required to constantly verify that such creative leaps are in fact rooted in the data.

6.4 Evaluating a GT

According to Glaser (1998), GT does not need to be assessed. It auto-assesses itself and has an intrinsic power to autocorrect. The characteristic *modifiability* of GT ensures that newly uncovered elements which 'disprove' the categories as they have been laid out in a GT do not actually falsify that theory. Since it is modifiable, such discoveries only mean that some categories of the theory are not saturated (anymore), that theoretical sampling needs to be reactivated and that further follow ups, and perhaps new data, are required to reformulate a more or less substantial part of the theory.

Besides its disputable auto-corrective power (Flick, 2018b), the fact that research exists in a specific scientific community means that it always undergoes assessment, and the assumptions underlying such assessment are not always agreed on nor coherent with the methodologies of qualitative research (Morse, 2003; Parahoo, 2003). Nevertheless, like it or not, all researchers, be they doctoral students or professional experts, are expected to produce research that meets the kind of assessment criteria in use in various areas: peer-reviewed academic journals, doctoral committees, assessors of research projects, procedures for assessing academic productivity and so on. In all of these areas any research study is legitimately required (although in reality it should be explicit *who* requires it and *for what purpose*) to meet certain key requirements. These include originality and significance of the research theme, connection of the research question to a set of knowledge acquired via the scientific literature on the theme, suitability of the chosen methods to the nature of the research question, criteria for selecting participants (sampling), the systematic nature of data collection and analysis, the traceability of the analysis in the data, and the distinction between data and interpretations. These requirements are joined by others which are more extrinsic to the nature of the research, requirements such as following ethical standards in the research (ethical considerations), ensuring the results are relevant and using a quality writing style.

GT in particular requires reshaping these general evaluation criteria in some ways, as they do not all make sense in relation to GT research. It also imposes other assessment criteria specifically linked to the nature of the method. Such criteria should be adopted by those tasked with assessing a study for a doctoral exam (defence or *viva*), a peer-reviewed publication or funding; indeed, they can be especially useful for self-assessing one's own work or, more simply, critically reading a scientific article. Some otherwise-universally accepted evaluation criteria have no meaning in relation to GT. Take sampling, for example. How can theoretical sampling be judged in terms of being sufficiently representative to allow generalizations?

In fact, assessing research that produces a theory is paradigmatically different from assessing research that experimentally verifies a set of hypotheses. In the latter, assessment consists of verifying whether or not the procedures were implemented correctly; the significance of the results is only marginally evaluated. In contrast, assessing research that produces a theory requires the difficult task of verifying both whether the results are truly derived from the data, and whether the theory has 'grip', coherence and suitability, that is, its ability to hold up against counterarguments, not to mention its theoretical power to say something that is relevant for someone. Meaningful evaluation criteria for this method cannot be expressed in the form of objectively measurable parameters. They can, however, be expressed effectively in the form of questions, that is points of attention which are useful especially for self-evaluating the rigour and significance of the results. Borrowing from Glaser (1998), the three fundamental features of GT – fit, relevance and work – could thus represent three criteria for evaluating the research outcomes. I particularly appreciate this participant-oriented perspective for assessing the value of research and its 'validity', an approach in which relevance is closely related to workability. For research in a practical field, such as education, nursing, marketing and computer science, this is a pivotal criterion. However, other extrinsic criteria should be taken into account for external evaluation as well. This is why second-generation grounded theorists have provided checkpoints (Corbin & Strauss, 2015) and criteria (Charmaz, 2014) for assessing GT specifically.

To summarize the various approaches, especially for self-evaluating one's own process, I would recommend reviewing the process through the following questions. Such a technique is helpful because questions are better than objective criteria in representing the purpose of qualitative assessment:

- *Theoretical sampling*. How was the sample selected? How did the theoretical sampling proceed? Are the data sufficient to support the inferences produced? Is saturation justified (explanation of saturation)?
  - *Credibility*. Are there enough data and systematic comparison, enough evidence and links between data and arguments?

- *Traceability of the process.* Were the categories generated empirically? Is the process of generating the categories traceable or transparent? Are the categories carefully described? Is it possible to retrace the main events that indicated the categories? Are there sound (logical) links between the analysis conducted and the data collected? Is there sufficient empirical evidence to allow the reader to agree with the analysis?
- *Integration of the theory.* Are the concepts systematically linked? Are the categories adequately developed? How and why has the core category been selected, based on which criteria?
- *Depth.* Does the theory generated here account for the phenomenon under investigation in its totality? Are the findings creatively presented? Has the research succeeded only in identifying marginal aspects or taken meanings for granted? Are the results linked to the current scientific debate on this theme?
- *Relevance.* Do the categories and proposed process give rise to new perspectives? Are they meaningful? Do they challenge consolidated knowledge on the theme? Are they conceptually dense? Do they have strong explanatory power? Will the theory or the concepts presented here last over time? Do they lead to new research?
- *Usefulness.* Does the theory make sense for the participants? Does it offer interpretations that are applicable for the practitioners? Does it tap into relevant questions in the professional debate? Does it suggest directions for change and innovation?

To Sum Up

- The tools essential for the analysis include memos, illustrated here in their analytical and meta-cognitive functions, and diagrams and storylines, which are the specular tools for integrating the theory.
- The report writing is a further moment of theorization because theory is not the product of writing but instead takes shape within the writing process. Writing up GT is a communicative project that requires a careful and functional choice of content.
- The ninth and last step of the GT journey is evaluation. After reflecting on the role of assessment in research of this type, a list of questions for self-assessment is provided (instead of a grid of objectively valid criteria).

Further Readings

On Memo Writing

Charmaz, K. (2014). *Constructing Grounded Theory: A Practical Guide through Qualitative Analysis*, 2nd edn. London: Sage, chap. 7.

Glaser, B. (1978). *Theoretical Sensitivity*. Mill Valley, CA: Sociology Press, chap. 5.

Maps and Diagrams

Bryant, A. (2017). *Grounded Theory and Grounded Theorizing: Pragmatism in Research Practice*. New York: Oxford University Press, chap 10.

Clarke, A. (2005). *Situational Analysis: Grounded Theory after the Postmodern Turn*. Thousand Oaks, CA: Sage.

Strauss, A., & Corbin, J. M. (1998). *Basics of Qualitative Research: Grounded Theory Procedures and Techniques*, 2nd ed. Newbury Park: Sage, chap. 14.

GT Evaluation

Charmaz, K. (2011). Grounded Theory Methods in Social Justice Research. In N. K. Denzin, & Y. Lincoln (Eds.), *The Sage Handbook of Qualitative Research*, 4th ed. Los Angeles: Sage, 359–80.

Corbin, J., & Strauss, A. (2015). *Basics of Qualitative Research: Techniques and Procedures for Developing Grounded Theory*, 4th ed. Thousand Oaks, CA: Sage, cap 16.

Writing

Charmaz, K. (2014). *Constructing Grounded Theory: A Practical Guide through Qualitative Analysis*, 2nd ed. London: Sage, chap 11.

Corbin, J., & Strauss, A. (2015). *Basics of Qualitative Research: Techniques and Procedures for Developing Grounded Theory*, 4th ed. Thousand Oaks, CA: Sage, cap 17.

Gibson, B., & Hartman, J. (2014). *Rediscovering Grounded Theory*. London: SAGE, chap. 13.

Urquhart, C. (2013). *Grounded Theory for Qualitative Research: A Practical Guide*. Los Angeles: Sage, chap. 8.

Conclusions: Theoretical Sensitivity as a Virtue

Cultivating Your Own Theoretical Sensitivity

Is GT for everyone? Is it a procedural mechanism that anyone who masters the method can successfully apply? Or does it require innate capabilities that makes using this methodology the prerogative of a few? Are *grounded theorists* born or made? GT 'devotees', sometimes seen as a bit of a sect (Greckhamer & Koro-Ljungberg, 2005), tend to patronize other methods by presenting this one as an esoteric art form many but not everyone can master, similar to the ability to produce art with a musical instrument. According to this cultic view, the element that makes this a method esoteric is *theoretical sensitivity*, that nearly elusive virtue I have referenced several times in the course of this book.

In the final pages of this journey I will begin by addressing whether theoretical sensitivity is innate or can be learnt and cultivated before exploring its distinctive characteristics. It would be reductive to disregard the fact that having a natural disposition for this type of analysis does play a role, combined with a sort of 'faith'; that is, *believing* that this method 'works'.

Significantly enough, Glaser's main work (1978) actually takes its name from the concept of theoretical sensitivity. There is no doubt that mechanically mastering GT techniques and procedures without theoretical sensitivity would be sterile, producing only superficial and trivial theories. However, research practice and the willingness to adopt and exercise certain heuristic stances can unquestionably contribute to refining and enhancing a person's theoretical sensitivity. Strauss and Corbin (1990, chapter 6) have suggested some 'behavioural' techniques to increase this capacity. While their attempt is valuable and noteworthy, it is frankly difficult to argue that this skill can be learnt by mechanically repeating simple exercises and applying techniques. Instead, it is useful to understand the components that constitute theoretical sensitivity and, more generally, what abilities the researcher must be ready to cultivate in doing GT. I have identified six basic ingredients:

1) *Being able to live in the chaos.* It is impossible to eliminate confusion, uncertainty or disorder; we have to live in it. And yet living with complexity and disorder is not easy.

As Glaser wrote (1998, p. 50), the 'researcher has to tolerate regression and confusion – feeling stupid, young, out of control and like one doesn't know anything. This can kill motivation by feeling like one is going crazy by being unable to see what is going on'. Glaser alleviates this anxiety with the somewhat positivist confidence that, because social reality is structured by patterns, sooner or later these patterns will unfold before the eyes of the regularly pacing scrupulous researcher. Not everyone shares his positivist optimism however, and often it is necessary to welcome anxiety, learning to manage it while waiting for some kind of light at the end of the tunnel.

A few years ago, I wrote in a GT research memo about the pedagogical model of teachers in a multicultural context (Tarozzi, 2006):

> Doing GT is like to reclaim a marsh. One continues to add sand without seeing any result. Then, suddenly, if you don't give up, something starts emerging, as a progressive accumulation, as a whole. It is not a matter of gradualness but of unexpected moments of enlightenment, that happen in an invisibly additional way. They create an accumulation that takes shape and it becomes theory.

I wrote this just after my core category had abruptly emerged following a long-lasting and chaotic theoretical coding period.

Since the spiral-shaped GT process does not unfold along just one seamless procedural track, while living in the darkness, we must be prepared to cope with the unexpected. GT users thus need both wide-ranging flexibility (to not be guided by rigid and dogmatic perspectives) and enduring perseverance (to keep going when everything seems unworkable and vain).

2) *Being able to suspend judgement.* This means adopting not only a non-prejudiced and sufficiently open stance towards the data but also an open willingness to listen, impartially and non-judgementally to the participants.

It is also an invitation to don the dress of the *epoché* (Tarozzi, 2005), that is, the epistemic act which according to phenomenology helps in the task of bracketing and accessing the heuristic process of authentic understanding. Bracketing is suspending one's assent with regard to a naive experience of the world, the assertions of the objective sciences with their criteria of truth and the very idea of objectively knowing reality as expressed by non-sensitizing concepts. In GT, *epoché* is applied to a number of cases: the requirements of funding bodies, the pre-existing literature, participants' expectations and coding labels.

3) *Intentionality*. According to phenomenology, this is the capacity of consciousness to make sense of the world. It is the natural inclination of subjective consciousness to tend towards the object. In conducting research, therefore, it can become an epistemic device that allows us to grasp the dimension of meaning and lived experience. GT practitioners must develop this competence and broaden their field of experience; they must augment their potential to grasp not the facts and things comprising objective reality, but rather meanings. In doing so, they may gain an authentic understanding of subjects, phenomena and situations.

4) *Caring for the relational dimension*. Since many diverse and fruitful meanings always bloom from relationships, being in a relationship and assuming the ethical and existential responsibility for it is pivotal in doing GT. Research is an exploration of the subjects' minds, thus calling on researchers to step outside themselves in order to access other people's experiences and engage personally with other people's existential dimensions. Ideally, research also involves the responsibility of understanding and adopting participants' main concern, thereby maintaining a constant and careful sensitivity towards the words and actions of participants. This sensitivity is not only an ethical requirement, it is also a powerful methodological opportunity to engage with rich data. Paying constant attention to the relational dimension and participants' main concern from the initial moment of negotiating access to the field until the final moment of sharing research findings is a key personal ability on the part of researchers, not to mention a crucial element that makes the GT relevant and functional.

5) *Ability to conceptualize*. This means thinking abstractly, theorizing, and philosophizing. This virtue is a hallmark of the method and I have already

talked extensively about it in Chapter 5. Here I would like to focus on conceptualization as an ability or even a virtue. Researchers who have been trained in empirical research, who come to GT by way of quantitative studies, have usually assimilated Wittgenstein's statement that 'whereof one cannot speak, thereof one must be silent' so deeply that they feel stuck when their own research must take off from description to conceptualization, a phase requiring speaking about precisely those things 'of which one must be silent'. Being well rooted in the data and thinking analytically on the basis of those data is also essential for GT, and researchers who are overconfident about theorization must be reminded of this fact. Nevertheless, speculative thinking is necessary if GT users are to abstract, synthesize and generate meanings. GT requires theorization and theoretical skills, a philosophical stance, in order to successfully move beyond description and conceptualize. Conceptual ability in GT is ultimately a form of philosophical thinking that requires the practitioner to apply the forms of abstract thinking to empirical research. This ability has practical consequences, such as producing not only highly analytical memos but also, as often happens to me, lengthy self-reflective memos which differ from descriptive or analytic ones. Self-reflection is a way of philosophizing, an inner dialogue that allows researchers to express themselves in the construction of the theory by interpreting the phenomena under inquiry.

6) *Cultivating insight and the logic of abduction*. This last ingredient deserves to be explained in more depth and its own separate paragraph for two reasons. First, because it is closely related to the conceptual pacing of this method's analytical process and the operation of the virtue of theoretical sensitivity that is needed to guide it. Secondly, because intuition, creativity or imaginative thinking are not always recognized as fundamental skills for good researchers; rather, they are often expected to stick close to the data and keep their creativity under wraps.

Consider this part of a memo I wrote some years ago while I was theoretically coding my data as part of research exploring processes of family television governance (Tarozzi, 2007) with preschool children.

> This morning I woke up with clear goals. After the umpteenth session of coding interviews and observations, I decided to devote this morning to analytical thinking, to conceptualisation: I'm very determined to find a general model which 'holds up'. I re-read my

> memos, my first working paper, my code tree [the nodes catalogue generated with the software NVivo] and I sketched few signs on a piece of paper. For a while I chased my own tail, not reaching anything, then, as if by magic, enlightenment pushed me to sketch the basic diagram of my theory. It's beautiful, it's effective, it says really something new. Everything is very exciting. I feel a dense, deep, calm joy. (30.7.05)

In the large majority of established research traditions, imaginative thinking and guessing is considered to lie outside of research. It is something that simply happens, something that occurs to us regardless of our intentionality.

Insights are the primary source of every theorization. Glaser and Strauss, who concluded their seminal book with a chapter dedicated to the value and heuristic function of insight as a source of theory, claimed that insight can be achieved through systematic comparative analysis. They do not, however, explain how this can be rendered possible.

Insights occur suddenly; they surprise us in the most unexpected moments, seeming to come from faraway rather than forming part of us, part of our subjectivities. Yet there are strategies for cultivating them, or at least for not letting them escape when they do come looking for us and understanding how to take advantage of them in theory building.

This is particularly evident in the advanced stages of coding. Not surprisingly, the early steps of coding are conducted at a desk. Here, the analyst works with the transcripts in an intimate space without too many distractions because all of his or her attention must be focused on the details of the text to be coded. In contrast, the work of conceptualization in theoretical coding requires open and airy spaces. When the researcher's mind is totally absorbed in the coding processes during analysis, it is so entangled in a network of self-referential and sterile concepts as to risk analytical implosion. At this point I personally turn off the computer, put away the sheets of paper and transcriptions, and go outdoors. I need to suspend coding and step way back from analysis, to move my mind away, elsewhere. Over time I have realized that these interruptions create the space for insight to emerge. As illustrated by the memo quoted earlier, I need to move away from my desk, from my computer, my transcriptions and books and go outside, for a walk, a swim, a run or a mountain hike.

Personally, as I also narrated in a Corbin and Strauss book (2015, pp. 147–51), I find it particularly effective to take long hikes, especially in the mountains, and I encourage my students to do the same. Hiking not only provide the conditions for a mental space in which another type of thought can emerge and thereby widen the thinker's perspective but also has intense symbolic significance which, for me personally, has an extremely powerful effect. Following a trail to walk to a peak or other destination certainly entails the effort of going uphill and following a marked path, an effort similar to that of following a research procedure (although detours are always possible and often pleasant). If the goal is a summit, however, the reward for your effort also involves reaching a viewpoint that opens onto a different, wider horizon. Changing the perspective used to look at things and opening up a new horizon for the gaze is a useful exercise of conceptualization that helps to bring out divergent thinking. It helps the analyst to think big; it favours the emergence of profound thoughts or wide-ranging synthesis and the construction of far-reaching speculative scenarios.

Once we have made room in our minds, shifting our attention to something other than coding, insight can emerge. Insight happens when we need to make sense of materials that do not fit into pre-established categories, to make sense of something dissonant or irregular, such as negative cases. It also comes into play when we observe something vague and incomprehensible that needs explaining.

According to Glaser and Strauss (1967), insights emerge from systematic comparative analysis, and so we have to endorse the associative way of thinking that is typically the form of creative thinking. Imaginative or creative thinking is stimulated by surprise and wonder, which are in turn features of metaphorical thinking (Locke, 2007), or by serendipity (Merton & Barber, 2004; Konecki, 2008), the happenstance of discovering something important while seeking something else. Indeed, scholars have recently recognized the role of serendipity in GT (Bryant & Charmaz, 2007). Glaser and Strauss refer to this as an 'unanticipated, anomalous, and strategic finding that gives rise to a new hypothesis' (1967, p. 2).

Even more than serendipity, what favours the emergence of insight is an associative way of thinking that allows the researcher to create links among distant phenomena.

The competence of developing 'hunches' has to do with the ability to produce metaphors. According to eighteenth-century Italian philosopher Giambattista Vico (Verene, 1991; Vico, 1948), the ability to invoke metaphors belongs to the realm of imagination, which is defined as the eye of acumen (*ingenii oculos*). This capacity can combine remote phenomena and produce new knowledge as a result. Imagination thus allows GT researchers to facilitate constant comparison among data, categories, and properties, and entails GT's logic. This logic is quite unlike the 'naïve inductivism' (Haig, 1995) that too often describes the inferences generated in GT. On the contrary, it is much more similar to the abductive reasoning that has recently been widely recognized as the logic behind the GT method (Locke, 2007; Reichertz, 2019).

Archimedes and the Logic of Abductive Scientific Discovery

To sum up and illustrate this way of reasoning and the virtues needed to perform it as well as some features of theoretical sensitivity, I would like to recall the well-known story of Archimedes discovering the eponymous principle.

In Vitruvius's account, that discovery stemmed from an urgent concern: Hiero, the king of Syracuse in Sicily, commissioned a goldsmith to make a golden crown. Suspecting that the goldsmith might have replaced some of the gold he was given with an equally weighty quantity of less precious metal, however, Hiero asked Archimedes to try to resolve the question and so determine whether or not the crown was pure gold.

It was not enough to measure the crown's weight, since the craftsman could have replaced the gold with the same weight in other metals. It was necessary to instead calculate the volume of the crown in order to determine the density of the metal.

As a fine mathematician, Archimedes had discovered how to measure the volume of many irregular solids. That is why he must have seemed to Hiero the best person to measure the volume of such an irregularly shaped object as a crown in the form of a wreath. Moreover, Archimedes could not have said no to this ferocious tyrant nor failed to meet his expectations. It is easy to imagine him very nervous and stressed, under intense pressure and looking for a brilliant solution that might have elevated his reputation even while fearing the fatal consequences of failure. Vitruvius tells us that Archimedes, perhaps to curb his anxiety, left his laboratory and went to the public bath in Syracuse looking for some relaxation.

Once at the public bath in Syracuse, the mathematician immersed himself in a tub, being careful not to make the water spill over the edges. As we know, however, the water overflowed anyway.

He paused for a moment; thoughts quickly crossed his mind, rapid associations occurred and, finally, he shouted his famous phrase: 'EUREKA! I have found it!'. He guessed that the volume of spilled water was equal to the volume of his body under water. He realized that he could determine the gold content of the crown by measuring the water it would displace in a bowl against the amount of water displaced by a lump of gold weighing the same as the crown. He could thus tell Hiero whether the goldsmith was honest. He was so excited that he raced naked down the street towards Hiero's palace.

The logic of Archimedes's discovery is emblematic for illustrating a typical means of theory building in GT and, in particular, the role creativity and imagination play in this process.

Insight linking distant phenomena almost always appears by abandoning the coding work to turn our attention to something different. The story could teach us that there are two key elements in creating the space for insight to emerge. First, being under pressure definitely helps – deadlines, funding bodies, pressure from supervisors and so on, contribute to concentrating the creative effort. Would Archimedes ever have discovered the principle of the physics if he had not felt the tyrant Hiero breathing down his neck? It is important to always carry our research problem with us, having it worry us from the moment we wake up to the moment we go to bed. However, it also important to step back from analysis and move mind away, to leave the lab or office and to go to the bath or somewhere else, outdoors.

There is another element that suggests something about the right conditions for insight to emerge. Archimedes also had a weighty ethical responsibility in that he was somehow responsible for condemning the craftsman. He performed the test, the artisan's fraud was revealed and therefore the goldsmith was executed. It could be argued that ethical responsibility further increases pressure, and thereby creates the mental space for the emergence of insight.

Following the abductive reasoning that produces probable conclusions, beginning from a premise that is certain but not true, GT advocates creative, relevant and non-tautological (since its minor premise is only probable) thinking. In this probability there is space for discovering something new, unfathomed and unknown. Here lies GT's unique feature of introducing any new ideas through a rigorous research process.

For insight to appear, some fortuitous event, unexpected episode or enlightening incident such an immersion in Syracuse's public tub is needed. And yet this is not enough. Many people prior to Archimedes had climbed into the same tubs before. Since abductive reasoning is fruitful and generates a conjecture or insight, it requires the creation of a rational horizon in which guesses, conjecture and hunches can acquire meaning. It requires a background against which a figure can stand out. The analyst then needs acumen which, through abductive reasoning, is capable of grasping this sign, transforming it into a theoretical hypothesis and, finally, checking if it is rooted in the data.

To conclude, let me offer a final consideration. GT does not stop with the elaboration of conjectures or production of insights. Rather, it requires a laborious task of theory construction that embodies two processes: one, securely grounding the conjectures that have emerged through insight in the data so as to guarantee the empirical foundation of the emerging theory; and, two, systematically and synthetically constructing an integrated theory, encompassing intentionally interpretive elements, that is capable of conceptually explaining what is happening in the context being analysed.

Theoretical sensitivity is the ability to conceptualize and think about data in theoretical terms, a process involving both irrational and rational characteristics, inductive and deductive logic, creativity and rigour: two complementary movements nicely synthesized by Glaser and Strauss when they stress the importance of having 'theoretical insight, combined with the ability to make something with this'.

The GT journey is adventurous and cautious at the same time. It is made of intense experiences and sudden enlightenment, but also of patient and monotonous clerical work, of unexpected revelatory leaps and slow progressions to provide a rational account of what happened.

To Sum Up

This chapter has addressed the skill of theoretical sensitivity, and its main ingredients or components have been outlined – being able to live in the chaos, the ability to conceptualize, being able to suspend judgement, making sense, the caring-relational dimension and cultivating insight.

Insight and imaginative thinking are explored in GT in particular by showing their implications in the logic of scientific 'discovery' and their meaning within GT.

Further Readings

On Theoretical Sensitivity

Gibson, B., & Hartman, J. (2014). *Rediscovering Grounded Theory*. London: SAGE, chapter 6.

Kelle, U. (2005), 'Emergence' vs 'Forcing' of Empirical Data? A Crucial of 'Grounded Theory' Reconsidered. *Forum Qualitative Sozialforschung*, 6 (2). Art. 27.

Kelle, U. (2007). The Development of Categories: Different Approaches in Grounded Theory. In A. Bryant, & K. Charmaz (Eds.), *The SAGE Handbook of Grounded Theory*. Los Angeles: Sage, 191–213.

On Abduction

Carson, D. (2009). The Abduction of Sherlock Holmes. *International Journal of Police Science & Management*, 11,193–202

Locke, K. (2007). Rational Control and Irrational Free-play: Dual-thinking Modes as Necessary Tension in Grounded Theorizing. In A. Bryant & K. Charmaz (Eds.), *The SAGE Handbook of Grounded Theory*. London: Sage, 565–79.

Reichertz, Jo (2010). Abduction: The Logic of Discovery of Grounded Theory. *Forum Qualitative Sozialforschung*, 11 (1).

Reichertz, J. (2019). Abduction: The Logic of Discovery of Grounded Theory – An Updated Review. In A. Bryant, & K. Charmaz (Eds.), *The SAGE Handbook of Current Developments in Grounded Theory*. Los Angeles, CA: SAGE, 259–81.

On Serendipity

Merton, R. K., & Barber, E. G. (2004). *The Travels and Adventures of Serendipity: A Study in Historical Semantics and the Sociology of Science*. Princeton: Princeton University Press.

Konecki, K. T. (2008). Grounded Theory and Serendipity: Natural History of a Research. *Qualitative Sociology Review*, 4 (1), 171–86.

References

Aldiabat, K. M., & Le Navenec, C. L. (2011). Philosophical Roots of Classical Grounded Theory: Its Foundations in Symbolic Interactionism. *The Qualitative Report*, 16 (4), 1063–80.

Amankwaa l.c. (2005), Maternal Postpartum Role Collapse as a Theory of Postpartum Depression. *The Qualitative Report*, 10 (1), 21–38.

Bailey, K. D. (2008). *Methods of Social Research*. New York: The Free Press (or. Ed. 1982).

Baker, C., West, J., & Stern, P. (1992). Method Slurring; The Grounded Theory/Phenomenology Example. *Journal of Advanced Nursing*, 17 (11), 1355–60.

Benoliel, J. Q. (1996). Grounded Theory and Nursing Knowledge. *Qualitative Health Research*, 6 (3), 406–28.

Blumer, H. (1954). What Is Wrong with Social Theory? *American Sociological Review*, 18, 3–10.

Blumer, H. (1969). *Simbolic Interactionism*. Englewood Cliffs, NJ: Prentice Hall.

Bowen, G. A. (2006). Grounded Theory and Sensitizing Concepts. *International Journal of Qualitative Methods*, 5 (3), Article 2.

Bowon, K. (2013). Competitive Priorities and Supply Chain Strategy in the Fashion Industry. *Qualitative Market Research: An International Journal*, 16 (2), 214–42.

Birks, M., & Mills, J. E. (2012). *Grounded Theory: A Practical Guide*. Los Angeles: Sage.

Bryant, A. (2003). A Constructive/ist Response to Glaser. *Forum Qualitative Sozialforschung / Forum: Qualitative Social Research*, 4 (1), Art. 15.

Bryant, A. (2009). Grounded Theory and Pragmatism: The Curious Case of Anselm Strauss. *Forum Qualitative Sozialforschung / Forum: Qualitative Social Research*, 10 (3), 1–31.

Bryant, A. (2017). *Grounded Theory and Grounded Theorizing: Pragmatism in Research Practice*. New York: Oxford University Press.

Bryant, A., & Charmaz, K. (2007). *The SAGE Handbook of Grounded Theory*. Los Angeles, CA: SAGE.
Burawoy, M. (1991). Reconstructing Social Theories. In M. Burawoy, J. Gamson, J. Schiffman, A. Burton, A. A. Ferguson, L. Salzinger et al. (Eds.), *Ethnography Unbound: Power and Resistance in the Modern Metropolis*. Berkeley: University of California Press, 8–28.
Buscaglioni, L. (2013). *Grounded Theory: Il metodo, la teoria, le tecniche*. Firenze: Bonanno.
Charmaz, K. (1973). *Time and Identity: The Shaping of Selves of the Chronically Ill*, PhD dissertation, University of California, San Francisco.
Charmaz, K. (1987). Struggling for a Self: Identity Levels of the Chronically Ill. In J. A. Roth, & P. Conrad (Eds.), *Research in the Sociology of Health Care, vol. 6: The Experience and Management of Chronic Illness*. Greenwich, CT: JAI Press, 283–321.
Charmaz, K. (1991). *Good Days, Bad Days: The Self in Chronic Illness and Time*. New Brunswick, NJ: Rutgers University Press.
Charmaz, K. (1995). Grounded Theory. In J. Smith, R. Harré, & I. Lagenhoveluk (Eds.), *Rethinking Methods in Psychology*. London: Sage, 27–49.
Charmaz, K. (2000). Grounded Theory: Objectivist and Constructivist Methods. In N. Denzin, & Y. Lincoln (Eds.), *Handbook of Qualitative Research*, 2nd ed. Thousand Oaks, CA: Sage, 506–35.
Charmaz, K. (2001). Qualitative Interviewing and Grounded Theory Analysis. In Jaber F. Gubrium, & James A. Holstein (Ed.), *Handbook of Interview Research: Context and Method*. Thousand Oaks, CA: Sage, 675–94.
Charmaz, K. (2005). Grounded theory in the 21st Century. Applications for Advancing social justice studies. In N. K. Denzin, & Y. S Lincoln (Eds.), *The Sage handbook of qualitative research, 3rd edition*. Thousand Oaks, CA: Sage, 507–35.
Charmaz, K. (2007). Constructionism and the Grounded Theory. In J. A. Holstein, & J. F. Gubrium (Eds.), *Handbook of Constructionist Research*. New York: Guilford Publications, 397–412.
Charmaz, K. (2011). Grounded Theory Methods in Social Justice Research. In N. K. Denzin, & Y. Lincoln (Eds.), *The Sage Handbook of Qualitative Research*, 4th ed. Los Angeles: Sage, 359–80.
Charmaz, K. (2006). *Constructing Grounded Theory: A Practical Guide through Qualitative Analysis*. London: Sage.

Charmaz, K. (2009). Shifting the Grounds: Constructivist Grounded Theory Methods. In J. Morse et al. (Ed.), *Developing Grounded Theory: The Second Generation*. Walnut Creek: Left Coast (now Routledge, 2016), 127–54.

Charmaz, K. (2014). *Constructing Grounded Theory: A Practical Guide through Qualitative Analysis*, 2nd ed. London: Sage.

Charmaz, K. (2014b). Grounded Theory in Global Perspective: Reviews by International Researchers. *Qualitative Inquiry*, 20 (9), 1074–84.

Charmaz, K., & Mitchell R. G. (2001). Grounded Theory and Ethnography. In P. Atkinson et al. (Eds.), *Handbook of Ethnography*. London: Sage, 160–74.

Cheek, J. (2000). An Untold Story: Doing Funded Qualitative Research. In N. Denzin, & Y. Lincoln (Eds.), *Handbook of Qualitative Research*, 2nd ed. Thousand Oaks and London: Sage, 401–20.

Cheek, J. (2005). The Practice and Politics of Funded Qualitative Research. In N. Denzin, & Y. Lincoln (Eds.), *Handbook of Qualitative Research*, 3rd ed. Thousand Oaks and London: Sage, 387–409.

Choi, S., & Holroyd, E. (2007). The Influence of Power, Poverty and Agency in the Negotiation of Condom Use for Female Sex Workers in Mainland China. *Culture, Health & Sexuality*, 9 (5), 489–503.

Cisneros Puebla, C. A., Domínguez Figaredo, D., Faux, R., Kölbl, C., & Packer, M. (2006). Editorial: About Qualitative Research Epistemologies and Peripheries. *Forum Qualitative Sozialforschung / Forum: Qualitative Social Research*, 7 (4), Art. 4.

Clarke, A. (2003). Situational Analysis: Grounded Theory Mapping after the Postmodern Turn. *Symbolic Interaction*, 26 (4), 553–76.

Clarke, A. (2005). *Situational Analysis: Grounded Theory after the Postmodern Turn*. Thousand Oaks, CA: Sage.

Clarke, A. E., Friese, C., & Washburn, R. S. (2018). *Situational Analysis: Grounded Theory after the Postmodern Turn*. Los Angeles: Sage.

Clarke, A., & Charmaz, K. (Eds.) (2014). *Grounded Theory and Situational Analysis* (4 vol.). London: Sage.

Cohen, L., Manion, L., & Morrison, K. (2018). *Research methods in education*. 8th ed. London: Routledge.

Corbin, J., & Strauss, A. (2008). *Basics of Qualitative Research: Techniques and Procedures for Developing Grounded Theory: Juliet Corbin*, 3rd ed. London: Sage Publications.

Corbin, J., & Strauss, A. (2015). *Basics of Qualitative Research: Techniques and Procedures for Developing Grounded Theory*, 4th ed. Thousand Oaks, CA: Sage.

Cohen, L., Manion, L., & Morrison, K. R. B. (2018). *Research Methods in Education*. 8th ed. London: Routledge.

Creswell, J. (2007). *Qualitative Inquiry and Research Design: Choosing among Five Traditions*, 2nd ed. Thousand Oaks, CA: Sage.

Creswell, J. W., & Clark, V. L. P. (2007). *Designing and Conducting Mixed Methods Research*. Thousand Oaks: Sage Publications.

Crotty, M. (2015). *The Foundations of Social Research: Meaning and Perspective in the Research Process*. London: Sage.

De Monticelli, R. (2007). The Phenomenological Devolution and the Emerge of Persons. *Encyclopaideia: Journal of Phenomenology and Education*, XI (22), 9–29.

Denzin, N. (1992). *Symbolic Interactionism and Cultural Studies*. Oxford: Blackwell.

Denzin, N. K., & Lincoln, Y. S. (Eds.) (1994). *Handbook of Qualitative Research*. Thousand Oaks: Sage.

Denzin, N., & Lincoln Y. (Eds.) (2000). *Handbook of Qualitative Research*, 2nd ed. Thousand Oaks-London: Sage.

Denzin, N., & Lincoln Y. (Eds.) (2005). *Handbook of Qualitative Research*, 3rd ed. Thousand Oaks-London: Sage.

Dey, I. (2007). *Grounding Grounded Theory: Guidelines for Qualitative Inquiry*. Bingley: Emerald (or. Ed. 1999).

Everall, R. D., Bostik, K. E., & Paulson, B. L. (2006). Being in a Safety Zone: Emotional Experiences of Suicidal Adolescents and Emerging Adults. *Journal of Adolescent Research*, 21 (4), 370–92.

Flick, U. (2018). *Doing Grounded Theory (Qualitative Research Kit)*. Los Angeles: Sage.

Flick, U. (2018b). *Managing Quality in Qualitative Research*. Los Angeles: Sage.

Fournier, S. (1998). Consumers and Their Brands: Developing Relationship Theory in Consumer Research. *Journal of Consumer Research*, 24 (March), 343–73.

Geertz, C., & [Darnton, R.] (2017). *The Interpretation of Cultures: Selected Essays*. New York: Basic Books (ed. or. 1973).

Gibbs, G. (2018). *Analysing Qualitative Data: The Sage Qualitative Research Kit*, 2nd ed. London: Sage.

Gibson, B., & Hartman, J. (2014). *Rediscovering Grounded Theory*. London: Sage.

Giorgi, A. (Ed.) (1985). *Phenomenology and Psychological Research*. Pittsburg: Duquesne University Press.

Giorgi, A., & Giorgi, B. (2003). The Descriptive Phenomenological Psychological Method. In P. Camic, J. Rhodes, & L. Yardley (Eds.), *Qualitative Research in Psychology: Expanding Perspectives in Methodology and Design*. Washington, DC: APA, 243–73.

Glaser, B. (1965). The Constant Comparative Method of Qualitative Analysis. *Social Problems*, 12, 436–45.

Glaser, B. (1978). *Theoretical Sensitivity*. Mill Valley, CA: Sociology Press.

Glaser, B. (1992). *Basics of Grounded Theory Analysis*. Mill Valley, CA: Sociology Press.

Glaser, B. (1998). *Doing Grounded Theory: Issues and Discussions*. Mill Valley, CA: Sociology Press.

Glaser, B. (2001). *The Grounded Theory Perspective: Conceptualization Contrasted with Description*. Mill Valley, CA: Sociology Press.

Glaser, B. (2003). *The Grounded Theory Perspective ii: Description's Remodelling of Grounded Theory Methodology*. Mill Valley, CA: Sociology Press.

Glaser, B. (2007). Doing Formal Theory. In A. Bryant, & K. Charmaz (Eds.), *The Sage Handbook of Grounded Theory*. Los Angeles: Sage, 97–113.

Glaser, B. G. (2009). *Jargonizing: Using the Grounded Theory Vocabulary*. Mill Valley, CA: Sociology Press.

Glaser, B. [with the assistance of Holton, J.] (2004). Remodeling Grounded Theory. In *Forum Qualitative Sozialforschung / Forum: Qualitative Social Research*, 5 (2), Art. 4.

Glaser, B. G., & Strauss, A. L. (1965). *Awareness of Dying*. Chicago: Aldine de Gruyter.

Glaser, B. G., & Strauss, A. L. (1968). *Time for Dying*. Chicago: Aldine de Gruyter.

Glaser, B. G., & Strauss, A. L. (1967). *The Discovery of Grounded Theory: Strategies for Qualitative Research*. Chicago: Aldine de Gruyter.

Glaser, B. G., & Strauss, A. L. (1971). *Status Passage: A Formal Theory*. Chicago: Aldine de Gruyter.

Glaser, B., & Tarozzi, M. (2007). Forty Years after Discovery: Grounded Theory worldwide. Barney Glaser in Conversation with Massimiliano Tarozzi. *The Grounded Theory Review*, Special issue, November, 21–41.

Gobo, G. (2005). Ricerca qualitativa e sociologia. In Dovigo (Ed.), *La qualità plurale. Sguardi transdisciplinari sulla ricerca qualitativa*. Milano: Franco Angeli, 65–82.

Greckhamer, T., & Koro-Ljungberg, M. (2005). The Erosion of a Method: Examples from Grounded Theory. *International Journal of Qualitative Studies in Education*, 18 (6), 729–50.

Guba, E. G. & Lincoln, Y. S. (1994). Competing paradigms in qualitative research. In N. K. Denzin, & Y. S. Lincoln (Eds.), *Handbook of Qualitative Research*, 2nd ed. Thousand Oaks: Sage, 105–17.

Gubrium J. F., & Holstein J. A. (Eds.) (2001). *Handbook of Interview Research: Context and Method*. Thousand Oaks, CA: Sage.

Haig, B. D. (1995). Grounded Theory as Scientific Method. *Philosophy of Education*, 28 (1), 1–11.

Henwood, K., & Pidgeon, N. (1996). Grounded Theory in Psychological Research. In P. Camic, J. Rhodes, & L. Yardley (Eds.), *Qualitative Research in Psychology: Expanding Perspectives in Methodology and Design*. Washington DC: APA, 131–55.

Holton, J. (2007). The Coding Process and Its Challenges. In A. Bryant, & K. Charmaz (2010). *The Sage Handbook of Grounded Theory*. Thousand Oaks, CA: Sage, 265–89.

Holton, J. A., & Walsh, I. (2017). *Classic Grounded Theory: Applications with Qualitative and Quantitative Data*. Los Angeles: Sage.

Honey, A., & Halse, C. (2007). Looking after Well Siblings of Adolescent Girls with Anorexia: An Important Parental Role. *Child Care, Health and Development*, 33 (1), 52–8.

Hood, J. C. (2007). Orthodoxy vs. Power: The Defining Traits of Grounded Theory. In A. Bryant, & K. Charmaz (Eds.), *The SAGE Handbook of Grounded Theory*. Thousand Oaks, CA: Sage, 151–64.

Hsiung, P.-C. (2012). The Globalization of Qualitative Research: Challenging Anglo-American Domination and Local Hegemonic Discourse. *Forum Qualitative Sozialforschung / Forum: Qualitative Social Research*, 13 (1), Art. 21.

Husserl, E. *Ideas: General Introduction to Pure Phenomenology*. Translated by W. R. Boyce Gibson. London: George Allen & Unwin Ltd., 1982. Original edition 1913.

Inaba, M., & Kakai, M. (2019). Grounded Text Mining Approach: A Synergy between Grounded Theory and Text Mining Approaches. In A. Bryant, & K. Charmaz (Eds.), *The SAGE Handbook of Current Developments in Grounded Theory*. London: Sage, 332–51.

Kuhn, T. S. (1996). *The Structure of Scientific Revolutions*, 3rd ed. Chicago, IL: University of Chicago Press (or. ed. 1962).
Lincoln, Y., & Guba, E. (1985). *Naturalistic Inquiry*. Beverly Hills, CA: Sage.
Guba, E. G., & Lincoln, Y. S. (1994). Competing Paradigms in Qualitative Research. In N. K. Denzin, & Y. S. Lincoln (Eds.), *Handbook of Qualitative Research*. Thousand Oaks, CA: Sage, 105–17.
Hildenbrand, B. (2007). Mediating Structure and Interaction in Grounded Theory. In A. Bryant, & K. Charmaz (Eds.), *The SAGE Handbook of Grounded Theory*. Los Angeles: Sage, 539–64.
Kelle, U. (2005), 'Emergence' vs 'Forcing' of Empirical Data? A Crucial of 'Grounded Theory' Reconsidered. *Forum Qualitative Sozialforschung*, 6 (2). Art. 27.
Kelle, U. (2007). The Development of Categories: Different Approaches in Grounded Theory. In A. Bryant, & K. Charmaz (Eds.), *The SAGE Handbook of Grounded Theory*. Los Angeles: Sage, 191–213.
Konecki, K. T. (2008). Grounded Theory and Serendipity: Natural History of a Research. *Qualitative Sociology Review*, 4 (1), 171–86.
Konecki, K. T. (2011). Visual Grounded Theory: A Methodological Outline and Examples from Empirical Work. *Revija za Sociologiju*, 41, 131–60.
Lancy, D. F. (1993). *Qualitative Research in Education: An Introduction to the Major Traditions*. New York: Longman.
Locke, K. (2007). Rational Control and Irrational Free-play: Dual-thinking Modes as Necessary Tension in Grounded Theorizing. In A. Bryant, & K. Charmaz (Eds.), *The SAGE Handbook of Grounded Theory*. London: Sage, 565–79.
Lofland, J., & Lofland, L. H. (1984). *Analyzing Social Settings: A Guide to Qualitative Observation and Analysis*, 2nd ed. Belmont, CA: Wadsworth.
Lopez, V. A., & Emmer, E. T. (2000). Adolescent Male Offenders: A Grounded Theory Study of Cognition, Emotion and Delinquent Crime Context. *Criminal Justice and Behavior*, 27 (3), 292–311.
Lull, J. (1990). *Inside Family Viewing: Ethnographic Research on Television's Audience*. London-New York: Comoedia Book, Routledge.
Marton, F. (1986), Phenomenography: A Research Approach to Investigating Different Understandings of Reality. In P. Fetterman (Ed.), *Qualitative Approaches to Evaluating Education*. New York: Praeger.
May, K. (Ed.) (1996). Advances in GT. *Qualitative Health Research*, 6 (3), 309–441.

Mead, G. H., (2015). *Mind, Self, and Society: The Definitive Edition* (with Huebner, D. R., Joas, H., & Morris, C. W.). Chicago: University of Chicago Press (Or. Ed. 1934).

Mey, G. & Dietrich, M. (2016). Vom Text zum Bild – Überlegungen zu einer visuellen Grounded-Theory-Methodologie [From Text to Image—Shaping a Visual Grounded Theory Methodology]. *Forum Qualitative Sozialforschung / Forum: Qualitative Social Research*, 17(2), Art. 2.

Mey, G., & Mruck, K. (Eds.) (2011). *Grounded Theory Reader*. Wiesbaden: Springer.

McDonald, M. (2001). Finding a Critical Perspective in Grounded Theory. In R. S. Schreiber, & Ph. N. Stern (Eds.), *Using Grounded Theory in Nursing*. New York Springer, 113–57.

Merton, R. K., & Barber, E. G. (2004). *The Travels and Adventures of Serendipity: A Study in Historical Semantics and the Sociology of Science*. Princeton: Princeton University Press.

Miles, M., & Huberman, M. (1994). *Qualitative Data Analysis*. Thousand Oaks: Sage.

Morley, D. (1986). *Family Television: Cultural Power and Domestic Leisure*. London: Sage.

Morse, J. M. (1994). Designing Funded Qualitative Research. In N. K. Denzin, & Y. S. Lincoln (Eds.), *Handbook of Qualitative Research*. Thousand Oaks, CA: Sage, 220–35.

Morse, J. M. (1995). The Significance of Saturation. *Qualitative Health Research*, 5 (2), 147–9.

Morse, J. M. (2009). *Developing Grounded Theory: The Second Generation*. Walnut Creek: Left Coast (now Routledge, 2016). Contributions by Morse, J. M., Stern, P. N., Corbin, J. M., Bowers, B., Charmaz, K., & Clarke, A. E.

Morse, J. M. (2015). Editorial: Data Were Saturated …. *Qualitative Health Research*, 25 (5), 587–8.

Morse, J. M., & Niehaus, L. (2016). *Mixed Method Design: Principles and Procedures*. London: Routledge.

Morse, J. M. (2001), Situating Grounded Theory within Qualitative Inquiry. In R. S. Schreiber, & Ph. N. Stern (Eds.), *Using Grounded Theory in Nursing*. New York: Springer, 1–15.

Morse, J. M. (2003). A Review Committee's Guide for Evaluating Qualitative Proposals. *Qualitative Health Research*, 13 (3), 833–51.

Morse, J., & Carter, B. (1996). The Essence of Enduring and Expressions of Suffering: The Reformulation of Self. *Scholarly Inquiry for Nursing Practice*, 10 (1, Spring), 43–60.

Morse, J., & Clark, L. (2019). The Nuances of Grounded Theory Sampling and the Pivotal Role of Theoretical Sampling. In A. Bryant, & K. Charmaz (Eds.), *The SAGE Handbook of Current Developments in Grounded Theory*. Los Angeles: Sage, 145–66.

Morse, J. M., & Field, P.-A. (1995). *Qualitative Research Methods for Health Professionals*. Thousand Oaks: Sage.

Morse, J. M., & Niehaus, L. (2009). *Mixed method design: Principles and procedures*. Walnut Creek, Calif: Left Coast Press.

Morse, J., & Richards, L. (2002). *Readme First: For a User's Guide to Qualitative Methods*. Thousand Oaks, CA: Sage.

Moustakas, C. (1994). *Phenomenological Research Methods*. Thousand Oaks, CA: Sage.

Mruck, K., Cisneros Puebla, C. A., & Faux, R. (2005). Editorial: About Qualitative Research Centers and Peripheries. *Forum Qualitative Sozialforschung / Forum: Qualitative Social Research*, 6 (3), Art. 49.

Parahoo, K. (2003). Square Pegs in Round Holes: Reviewing Qualitative Research Proposals. *Journal of Clinical Nursing*, 12, 155–7.

Park, R., & Burgess, E. W. (Eds.) (1921), *The City*. Chicago: University of Chicago Press.

Pressley, M. et al. (2006). A Portrait of Benchmark School: How a School Produces High Achievement in Students Who Previously Failed. *Journal of Educational Psychology*, 98 (2), 282–306.

Priya, K. R., & Prakash, A. (2015). Analysing Qualitative Data: A Grounded Theory Approach. In K. R. Priya, & A. K. Dalal (Eds.), *Qualitative Research on Illness, Well-being and Self-growth: Contemporary Indian Perspectives*. New Delhi: Routledge, 59–73.

Rausch J., & Hamilton M. (2006). Goals and Distractions: Explanations of Early Attrition from traditional University Freshmen. *The Qualitative Report*, 11 (2), 317–34.

Rennie, D. L. (2000). Grounded Theory Methodology as Methodical Hermeneutics. Reconciling Realism and Relativism. *Theory and Psychology*, 10 (4), 481–502.

Richardson, J. (1999). The Concept and Methods of Phenomenographic Research. *Review of Educational Research*, 69 (1), 53–82.

Rizzo, R. (1993). Vagueness in the Haight Ashbury: A Study of Asocialization. In B. Glaser (Ed.), *Examples of Grounded Theory: A Reader*. Mill Valley, CA: Sociology Press, 126–38.

Reichertz, J. (2007). Abduction: The Logic of Discovery of Grounded Theory. In A. Bryant, & K. Charmaz (Eds.), *The SAGE Handbook of Grounded Theory*. Los Angeles: Sage, 214–28.

Reichertz, J. (2009). Abduction: The Logic of Discovery of Grounded Theory [39 paragraphs]. *Forum Qualitative Sozialforschung / Forum: Qualitative Social Research*, 11 (1), Art. 13, http://nbnresolving. de/urn:nbn:de:0114-fqs1001135.

Reichertz, J. (2019). Abduction: The Logic of Discovery of Grounded Theory – An Updated Review. In A. Bryant, & K. Charmaz (Eds.), *The SAGE Handbook of Current Developments in Grounded Theory*. Los Angeles, CA: SAGE, 259–81.

Schraw, G., Wadkins, T., & Olafson, L. (2007). Doing the Things We Do: A Grounded Theory of Academic Procrastination. *Journal of Educational Psychology*, 99 (1), 12–25.

Schütze, F. (2008). The legacy of Germany today of Anselm Strauss' vision and practice of sociology. In N. K. Denzin (Ed.), *Studies in symbolic interaction*. Bingley, UK: Emerald. 103–23.

Silverman, D. (1993). *Interpreting Qualitative Data: Methods for Analysing Talk, Text and Interaction*. London: Sage.

Silverman, D. (2000). *Doing Qualitative Research*. London: Sage.

Stern, P. N. (1994). Eroding Grounded Theory. In J. Morse (Ed.), *Critical Issues in Qualitative Research Methods*. Thousand Oaks, CA: Sage.

Stern, P. N., & Porr, C. (2011). *Essentials of Accessible Grounded Theory*. Walnut Creek, CA: Left Coast Press.

Stern, P. N. (2009). In the Beginning Glaser and Strauss Created Rounded Theory. In J. Morse et al. *Developing Grounded Theory: The Second Generation*. Walnut Creek: Left Coast (now Routledge, 2016), 23–9.

Stern, P. N. (2012). Jeanne Quint Benoliel. *Qualitative Health Research*, 22, 1580–81.

Strauss, A. L. (1987). *Qualitative Analysis for Social Scientists*. Cambridge: Cambridge University Press.

Strauss, A., & Corbin, J. M. (1990). *Basics of Qualitative Research: Grounded Theory Procedures and Techniques*. Newbury Park: Sage.

Strauss, A., & Corbin, J. M. (1997). *Grounded Theory in Practice*. Los Angeles: Sage.

Strauss, A., & Corbin, J. M. (1998). *Basics of Qualitative Research: Grounded Theory Procedures and Techniques*, 2nd ed. Newbury Park: Sage.

Strübing, J. (2007). Research as Pragmatic Problem-solving: The Pragmatist Roots of Empirically-grounded Theorizing. In A. Bryant, & K. Charmaz (Eds.), *The SAGE Handbook of Grounded Theory*. Los Angeles: Sage, 580–601.

Tarozzi, M. (1998). *La mediazione educativa. "Mediatori culturali" tra uguaglianza e differenza*. Bologna: Clueb.

Tarozzi, M. (2005). Epoché. In P. Bertolini (Ed.), *Per un lessico di pedagogia fenomenologica*. Trento: Erickson, 103–18.

Tarozzi, M. (Ed.) (2006). *Il senso dell'intercultura. Ricerca sulle pratiche di accoglienza, intercultura e integrazione in Trentino*. Trento: Iprase.

Tarozzi, M. (2007). Il modello generale: processi di governance televisiva familiare. In M. Tarozzi (Ed.), *Il governo della tv. Etnografie del consumo televisivo in contesti domestici*. Milano: Franco Angeli, 41–73.

Tarozzi, M. (Ed.) (2007a), *Il governo della tv. Etnografie del consumo televisivo in contesti domestici*. Milano: FrancoAngeli.

Tarozzi, M. (2008). *Che cos'è la Grounded Theory*. Roma: Carocci.

Tarozzi, M. (2011). Translating Grounded Theory into Another Language: When Translating Is Doing. In V. Martin, & A. Gynnild (Eds.), *Grounded Theory: Philosophy, Method, and the Work of Barney Glaser*. Boca Raton, FL: Brown Walker Press, 161–75.

Tarozzi, M. (2013). How Does My Research Question Come About? The Impact of Funding Agencies in Formulating Research Questions. *The Qualitative Report*, 18 (102), 1–11.

Tarozzi, M. (2014). Translating and Doing Grounded Theory Methodology: Intercultural Mediation as an Analytic Resource. In A. Clarke, & K. Charmaz (Eds.), *Grounded Theory and Situational Analysis* (4 vol.). London: Sage, 3, 21–37.

Tarozzi, M. (2019). Coding and Translating: Language as a Heuristic Apparatus. In A. Bryant, & K. Charmaz (Eds.), *The SAGE Handbook of Current Developments in Grounded Theory*. Los Angeles: Sage, 186–205.

Tarozzi, M., & Mortari, L. (Eds.) (2010). *Phenomenology and Human Science Today*. Bucharest: Zeta Books.

Thomas, G., & James, D. (2006). Reinventing Grounded Theory: Some Questions about Theory, Ground and Discovery. *British Educational Research Journal*, 32 (6), 767–95.

Thornberg, R. (2012). Informed Grounded Theory. *Scandinavian Journal of Educational Research*, 56 (3), 243–59.

Thornberg, R., & Dunne, C. (2019). Literature Review in Grounded Theory. In A. Bryant, & K. Charmaz (Eds.), *The SAGE Handbook of Current Developments in Grounded Theory*. Los Angeles: Sage, 243–58.

Urquhart, C. (2013). *Grounded Theory for Qualitative Research: A Practical Guide*. Los Angeles: Sage.

Van den Hoonard, W. C. (1997). *Working with Sensitizing Concepts: Analytical Field Research*. London: Sage.

Verene, D. P. (1991). *Vico's Science of Imagination*. Ithaca: Cornell University Press.

Vico, G. B. (1948). *The New Science of Giambattista Vico*. Ithaca: Cornell University Press.

Index

www.ingramcontent.com/pod-product-compliance
Lightning Source LLC
Chambersburg PA
CBHW050714280326
41926CB00088B/3029